AN UNCOMMON

Journey

Leadership Lessons

From a Preschool Teacher Who Became A University President

Shirley Raines

 outskirts press

"Shirley Raines truly embodies the spirit of a leader – her upbringing on a West Tennessee farm and previous work as a preschool teacher were merely stepping stones to her path to become President of the University of Memphis. In each step of her journey, she lived the leadership tenets outlined in the book, sharing battle-tested advice, which led to her success in philanthropy, research, and academics. Her ability to fearlessly say yes and focus on strengths, both within herself and others, makes her a natural choice to narrate her experiences on leadership. Her leadership journey is extraordinary!"

Paula Myrick Short, Ph.D., Senior Vice Chancellor for Academic Affairs and Provost, University of Houston

"Shirley Raines is an inspiring pioneer leader who uses her voice to lead great projects, champion education, and create a positive culture for others to succeed."

Steve Cockram, Author, Speaker and Founder of GiANT Worldwide

"Shirley Raines was a model of trust and determination throughout her amazing career. Students, colleagues, and strategic partners knew they could trust Dr. Raines, and her determination to seek the best from every relationship had enormous impact on the individuals, institutions, and communities which she served."

R. Brad Martin, Chairman of the Board, Chesapeake Energy Corporation

"Personable, powerful, and prepared were the words we used to describe Dr. Shirley Raines at her induction ceremony for the Tennessee Women's Hall of Fame and to recognize her 12 years as President of the University of Memphis."

**Yvonne Wood, Vice Chair,
Tennessee Women's Economic Council Foundation**

"Whether in a boardroom or before 18,000 people at the FedEx Forum, Dr. Raines immediately connects with people. She embodies what leadership is – character, capability, and being a catalyst for positive change."

Thomas Kadien, Sr. Vice President, International Paper

This is more than just another book about *Leadership,* it's the *owner's manual.* Dr. Raines shares her inspirational story, which will entertain and educate just as she has done for decades.

Duane Cummings, CEO *Leadercast*

DEDICATION

To the family, friends, and colleagues who supported me throughout my leadership journey.

Special appreciation for their love and support to my husband, Robert Joseph Canady; son, Brian Scott Smith; grandchildren, Riley Marie and Bryson Overton Smith; brother, Carey Athel Raines; and to all we call family, including Marti Overton and Sandy Smith; and friend, Rebecca Isbell.

In loving memory of my parents and brother, Evelyn Irene Raines, James Athel Raines, and David Anthony Raines

PLEASE SEE ACKNOWLEDGMENTS IN APPENDIX 4

TABLE OF CONTENTS

Appendixes

PREFACE

I am a woman who became a university president and kept the job for a dozen years.

A lot of people have asked me how I did that. So now I will confess that I had a leg up. I was born into a sharecropper's family and learned a lot from my hard-working parents on that West Tennessee farm. Picking cotton by hand makes your back hurt, your hands bleed, and the sun is relentless. As a family, we had a goal to own a small farm, which we attained when I was in seventh grade. Picking cotton by hand, growing crops, raising cattle and a garden kept the bills paid and the family fed. No one had an expectation that college was in my future to attend, let alone a job in a university.

During my early career as a preschool teacher, my supervisor described me as "spunky." Much later in my career, at the University of Memphis, I was called a "steel magnolia." I believe that without those early life lessons on the farm, I could not have developed the spunk to endure or the uncommon fortitude of a steel magnolia.

I wrote this book to tell my stories and to inspire leaders, especially aspiring women leaders, who are wondering if they should take their next leadership step. I envision my readership to be primarily women because traditionally the path to leadership has been steeper for women than their male counterparts. It is my hope that all aspiring leaders will be open to the possibilities and say "yes" to leadership. It is a worthy goal.

Doors should open for more women leaders. While the majority of college students are women, only three out of ten of the nation's college and university presidents are women, up just four percent from 2011. In 2001 when I was appointed as president, the percentage of women presidents in both community colleges and universities was approximately 23%. In 2016, only eight percent of doctorate-granting institutions were led by women. I had the privilege of being one of those eight percent and serving for 12 years.

Among women leaders, stories about their professional lives are rare. Over the course of my career, I have been asked many questions about my life and leadership experiences. In this book, you are invited to follow with me on the path I took and see the challenges I faced as well as the lessons I learned along the way. There may be something here that convinces you of the rewards of saying "yes" to leadership.

MY LEADERSHIP STORY

My career spanned educational appointments from preschool teacher to university president. At every career juncture, there were dilemmas, uncertainty, and my own feelings to sort through.

When I became a university president, the first woman president at the University of Memphis, people were interested in my feelings and past experiences that prepared me for the role. Their questions also are part of what prompted this book.

One question I was asked often is: "What does it feel like to be the first woman president of the University of Memphis?" At the time, I usually replied, "I feel honored, privileged, and grateful." In reality, I believe a man or another woman would have the same response, but I doubt any man would be asked, "What does it feel like to be a man president?" Some women university presidents refuse to answer the question at all because they want to be thought of as the president of their university, not as the woman president. However, after a number of poignant experiences, my response is different. Being named the first woman president of the University of Memphis was very significant to me at the time I was appointed and took on greater meaning during those 12 years.

Often asked about the discrimination I encountered as a female leader, I could answer by telling many stories. But, this book is not about discrimination. It is about leadership lessons I learned along my career journey that might light the way for future women leaders.

WHY WRITE THIS BOOK NOW?

Now, I have the title of president emeritus, the designation awarded to me from the Tennessee Board of Regents and the Board of Trustees of the University of Memphis. Emerita, the female nomenclature, was not the designation they chose. Presently, I spend my time speaking to groups about leadership, my academic field of early childhood education, and quality education in general. I often facilitate meetings for higher education institutions, foundations, government entities, and for non-profits. On a one-to-one basis, throughout my career, women and men have consulted me about their career moves, problems in their institutions, and asked for suggestions for engaging their university in partnering with their communities. Often audience members ask me if I have a book about my life as a leader. Now, I can answer yes.

Chapter 1

THE FORMATIVE YEARS

LIFE ON THE FARM

You might suspect that the chances were slim that I would ever become a teacher, much less a university president. After all, no one in my family had attained education beyond high school, and my father was a farmer with an eighth-grade education.

When I was very young, from birth to seventh grade, my father was a sharecropper on a small cotton farm in West Tennessee. My brothers and I were expected to work alongside our parents. We picked cotton by hand until my senior year in high school when we could afford a mechanical picker. Farming is hard work. Chopping and picking cotton by hand were necessary for our family's livelihood. My father made the work light with his humor, but he could be stern if we lagged behind in our chores. He called the work on our farm "an honest living by the sweat of your brow." That experience taught me life-long lessons: diligence, persistence, and doing whatever it takes to get the job done.

We always had food to eat, but money was tight. After my dad was able to buy his own land to farm, he was proud of the accomplishment for the rest of his life. But, he was anxious about making enough money from the cotton crops, soybeans, and cattle to pay the mortgage and to get loans to fund the next year's crop. I learned the difference between needs and wants. Needs came first and some of the wants later, if there was money. Throughout my career, I have worked with budgets where the distinction between needs and wants had to be made. Those farm lessons were invaluable when I had to budget public funds and be responsible for donors' generous contributions.

My first home where my family lived until I was in the seventh grade.

The house our family moved into when my father bought a farm.

My mother was the oldest of 11 children, so I was the oldest grandchild. As her siblings married and had children, I was called on to help take care of the little ones. At the family gatherings on most weekends, my job was to keep the younger children entertained. We danced, sang, played school, and rocked the littlest babies.

My younger brothers, Carey and David, were two of the most creative and inventive people I ever knew. They could fix anything – cars, trucks, tractors, or almost any piece of equipment. If they did not know how to do something, they learned, often by trial and error. From them, I gained the important lesson of using need as a motivator to understand the problem, learn the mechanics, and be inventive. Also, because of necessity, they did not have the luxury of waiting to get the task done, nor did they allow the fear of failure to prevent them from fixing whatever needed repairing.

I have a lot of fond memories of my youth on the farm. But, chopping or hoeing cotton was not one of them. As we worked in the fields, my brothers and I would watch the airplanes fly overhead and wonder about their destinations. We knew they were flying in and out of Memphis. We wondered if we would ever be on one of those planes.

STORYTELLING

I come from a long line of storytellers who taught and entertained. My father could make a story come to life. He made the lions roar at Daniel when he told the Bible story of "Daniel in the Lion's Den." His late-night ghost stories were spine-tingling. He was probably best at every family reunion when he gathered a crowd to listen to his mostly true stories.

He was keen on everyone remembering our farm family roots and told tales about our ancestors. The hardship stories he told always contained funny segments about how our family made our work light and country life appealing. He relished the laughter he heard when he told descriptive farm stories. The most requested story was about "Queen," the old farm horse Dad rode 13 miles to the Strawberry Festival in Humboldt, Tennessee. He won a blue ribbon riding her and out-performed all those city slicker competitors who brought their horses in trailers.

Another favorite was about using some ugly old mules to pull out a fancy sports car stuck in the mud on our country road. One of his beautiful stories was about how Christmas was saved one year. He did not have a penny to his name and was buying groceries on credit. He had no money for "pretties," his word for toys. The hero of the story was a generous local merchant, Richard Freeman, who loaned my father $20, allowing my father to be Santa Claus.

Whatever the story, Dad always drew a crowd and left them begging for more. Often the same tales were told year after year. Early in life, I learned the power of stories to entertain and teach.

We can be greatly influenced by the stories told by loved one like my father, a famous person, or a powerful leader. If an inspirational minister tells stories, we may relate to them and perhaps find a metaphor or parable that applies to our lives. For example from childhood, I was influenced by the parable of the talents from the Bible. If we use our talents, they multiply, but if we fail to use them, the talents are diminished (Matthew 25:14-30).

Think of other stories we recall easily as the giant in the story of David and Goliath, a reminder that huge problems may occur, but we have the stones in our hands to conquer them. If someone cautions, "Don't cry wolf," the Aesop's fable "The Boy Who Cried Wolf" comes to mind. I once heard someone say, "We need a rabbit to jump-start this project, but we need a turtle to finish the race." Immediately, I visualized the Aesop fable, "The Tortoise and the Hare."

Kieran Egan of Simon Fraser University said, "The mind organizes best in story form." The great truths of civilization have been passed down for centuries in the Bible, the Torah, and other sacred texts, including the myths and legends of native peoples.

Stories permeate all cultures and remain an avenue to communicate values across generations and across cultures. Passing stories down from generation to generation enables us to learn moral and cultural values in entertaining and enlightening ways that remain alive in our minds.

While our experiences are different, if we share our stories with others and find some commonalities, we can learn from each other. When people from other cultures share their stories, we may find commonalities with them. We may learn that the insights, wisdom, and perspectives from other cultures also are relevant to us.

As learners, we are always processing new information and linking the unknown to the known. If we are wise, we reflect on the new information we are attempting to learn and relate it to our own experiences. We also try on new ways of thinking. We use our reflections on our past successes and mistakes, as well as the lessons of our history to make better judgments and decisions in the future. Sometimes, we must consider what has happened to us indirectly or what we may have experienced vicariously through a story. We imagine what we would do in the situation the speaker or the author describes.

From my family's stories, I began to appreciate the power of story in narrative or music form as a tool for transmitting knowledge and wisdom, as a context for discerning and communicating values, and as a way to internalize meaning at a deeper level.

CHURCH AND COMMUNITY

In our community, the "difference makers," the adults in the church and the community, gave us opportunities to be truly involved. We attended Crossroads Baptist Church, and occasionally, I played the piano for the small Methodist church across the road from the Baptist church.

Both our community's Baptist and Methodist churches involved the youth, especially the teenagers. We planned and led activities, such as Vacation Bible School, participated in business meetings, and visited shut-ins as members of the chicken soup brigade. We were expected to have fun, but we were expected to work. The work was done shoulder to shoulder with the adults until we were ready to take on leadership roles. A leadership lesson – allow the learners to lean on the leaders, the more experienced ones, until they are ready to lead.

I am thankful to the adults who gave me responsibilities in the church and community, and then suffered through my feeble attempts and helped me practice until I got it right. Their leadership lessons included planning, organizing, speaking in front of groups, speaking up for what we believed, and adapting.

While the lessons learned on the farm, in church, and the community, profoundly shaped my early life, I remained a little country girl trying to see my path ahead.

Later in life, I ran across this quotation by Joseph Campbell that resonated with me: "If you can see your path laid out in front of you, step by step, you know it's not your path. Your own path you make with every step you take. That's why it's your path."

School Days

Mother always said, "Get a good education. We don't know what the future will bring, but you are always going to need a good education." At that time, she was referring to a high school education. She graduated from high school and my father had an eighth grade education. He quit school to help my disabled grandfather on the farm.

I attended Bells School from first grade through twelfth and vividly remember lessons I learned along the way that stuck with me all my life.

*My first day of school walking down the
steps of our sharecropper farmhouse.*

My fifth grade teacher, Elizabeth Jackson, asked me to help a
classmate with his reading. That experience led to the realization
that I could teach someone to read and instilled in me a passion for
teaching. Ms. Jackson also enrolled the class in the Junior Audubon
Society and had the class make flags of many different countries
around the world. Studying nature and the global awareness she fos-
tered were significant because in my limited country upbringing,

thinking about foreign lands was rare. I learned that we must have an appreciation for our natural world and for global societies.

Mr. Bill Emerson taught me algebra and set me on a mathematics path to statistics later on at the University of Tennessee from Dr. W.W. Wyatt. Now, I collect data, organize statistical information, and think about its significance, but I would not have known how to accomplish this if it had not been for my solid mathematics education and my excellent statistics professor. While I understand the cold hard facts are not all that is involved in a decision, good decision makers must rely on the data.

Mr. Emerson also was my softball coach. He taught me another significant lesson: "Keep your eye on the ball." When I struck out three times in a softball game, he did not yell or scream, but he did say when I walked past him, "Remember, keep your eye on the ball."

Ms. Anna Wista Williams, my Latin teacher, was responsible for my first trip to then Memphis State University. We competed in the Latin Tournament held on the campus, which was organized by Nellie Angel Smith, head of the Languages department and dean of women. All the students from Bells High competed in both the individual and class competitions. I am sorry that I let Ms. Williams down on the individual competition, although we did win the class competition. I was so fascinated by the university that I must have forgotten some of the Latin phrases.

Ms. Williams was also the only English teacher at Bells High, and she had high expectations. I learned how to use correct grammar, construct sentences, compose my thoughts, and write essays. In my later career, I wrote 15 books, two photo journals for teachers, and two children's books. I'm still trying to reach those higher expectations to express well what is needed for a good report or for a delightful poem. As much as the mechanics of English composition, those lessons taught me the necessity for high standards.

My opportunities changed the day college recruiters came to Bells School. A recruiter from the University of Tennessee at Martin offered me a scholarship on the spot based on my academic ranking in my senior class. I was in the top ten. Considering the class only had 23 students, the honor hardly seems like an accomplishment; however, later I learned the principal, Mr. B. J. Crider, recommended me. The scholarship for $300 was not a competitive scholarship by today's standards, but receiving it was a turning point in my life.

My family and I did not know how scholarships worked. My hard-working dad thought I should forego the scholarship because I had not earned the $300. He wanted me to apply for a job in the frozen food factory where I had worked the previous summer. Mother, however, had different ideas. She visited the University of Tennessee at Martin and learned about college life and scholarships. When Mother returned home, she announced to Dad, my brothers, and me, "She's going to college."

Often, I have wondered if I would have found my way to college if those recruiters had chosen to skip our small high school. I am grateful that Mother investigated what having a scholarship meant. She was very intelligent. I'm sure if she had had the opportunities and financial means to attend college, she could have had her choice of professions. Later in life, she worked as an assistant in a law office, and I know she wanted to be a lawyer.

I had never dreamed of going to college until my friend Pat started talking about it. No one in my family had attended college, and it did not seem remotely likely that my brothers and I would leave a cotton farm destined for a college campus.

College

A new world opened to me in college, one I had to learn to navigate. During a difficult course in human physiology, I found myself failing. I took the course the next semester, but it looked like I would not improve my score much. Because I had always made A's in high school, I felt like a failure. Imagining the courses ahead of me to be even more difficult, I went home discouraged and planned to drop out of college. I stayed away for almost three weeks.

Then one of my professors, Ms. Pauline Glover, called me on the phone and said, "Shirley, I've missed you in class. Where have you been?" I told her about my plans to drop out because of the difficulty I was having getting a passing grade in the physiology class. She said, "I will help you." Keep in mind that she was a creative writing teacher, not a human physiology teacher. She convinced me to return to campus by saying, "If you are not in the dorm by Sunday night, I am coming to get you. What are the directions to your family's farm off Highway 412?" When she asked for directions, I knew she was serious. I returned to campus, got the help I needed, graduated and became a teacher. What would I have become if Pauline Glover had not called and helped me find a study group? I soon realized that I was not the only one struggling to learn the material.

I have told this story many times through the years. What a lesson for teachers and leaders in education about the profound effect they can have on the lives of students. Ms. Glover was the professor who saved me.

Summary of Early Life and Moving Forward

From my teachers and professors, I gained a strong knowledge base on which to build for later lessons in life. From Mr. Emerson and Dr. Wyatt, whether through algebra or statistics, I learned the importance of data for making informed decisions. I understand why I should keep my eyes on the ball. To be an effective leader, focus on the key information needed for your core purpose. From Ms. Williams and Ms. Glover, I learned that my development as a reader, writer, listener, and speaker with high standards is beneficial in life and in successful leadership.

My family connection to children all those years stayed with me and affected my college and career path. Now, it was my turn to try to make a difference. I wanted to help children achieve more than was expected of them. I looked for appointments in programs that made a difference in people's lives and increased their chances for better livelihoods. The work gave me satisfaction and led me to question many assumptions about poverty and our society.

The lessons learned early in life are valuable and continue throughout your life. Not every childhood situation is idyllic. Resolve to handle certain situations in your later life differently. Strive to emulate other behaviors. Don't forget your family, where you came from, and what it was that made you who you are.

My two brothers and me, David Raines (L) and Carey Raines (R)

WHO'S IN CHARGE?

As the oldest child in a farm family, my responsibilities included farm chores and taking care of my two younger brothers. They grew up to be fine men, but as children, they tried my patience, especially on school days. They got into a lot of mischief when I was supposed to be taking care of them. "Shirley, you are in charge," was a phrase I heard most mornings as Mother left for work in a hosiery mill.

When Mother left very early before breakfast, she did not tell her sons to listen to their big sister. Instead, she said, "Shirley, you're in charge." That meant I was to make sure they were ready for school in time for the bus, take care of them after school, and keep them out of trouble. Sometimes, I failed.

"You're In Charge" Takes on New Meaning

"You're in charge" also was the surprise statement the principal said to me when I landed a teaching job in Louisville, Kentucky. The school term had already begun at Watson Lane Elementary School, which is near Fort Knox military base. With no teacher's aide to help me, my job was to teach the 25 "X2" children who stared at me for directions. To make it even more challenging, the school was so crowded that we had double sessions, thus the "X2." I had one group of children in the morning and another in the afternoon. I loved them, learned from them, and had my first experiences teaching children whose parents were deployed overseas. The families were racked with distress and worried about where they would be stationed next. I was trying to survive the challenges of teaching so many children while still trying to be another significant person in their lives.

On the first day of school as the principal closed the door to my classroom, he declared, "You're in charge." Whenever I wondered what to do, whenever I was hesitant and not sure of my next step, the "You're in charge" statement pulled me to action and through a rough year in an overcrowded school.

I still have flashbacks of three of the children I struggled to teach. One was a frail little boy who was so shy he would not speak. Another was a boy who perpetually stole things from other children's belongings. A third was a hyperactive child who could not sit still. I had some minor breakthroughs with all three, but no major miracles. Isn't it intriguing that those we struggle to help are the ones we remember best? As Joseph Campbell said, "Where you stumble, there lies your treasure."

First Days on the Job: "She's in Charge"

Regardless of the situation, first days on the job make impressions that often last a lifetime. After teaching children for a few years in Kentucky, we moved to Oak Ridge, Tennessee, and I attended the

University of Tennessee at Knoxville to earn my master's degree in child development and early childhood education. After completing my master's, I was offered a position as the director of Head Start for Knox County Schools. My job was to direct a program serving about 300 children and families in 14 centers.

On my first day, I nervously drove to the Head Start office to meet the people who were expected to report to me. While driving there, I questioned why I had accepted this position. How could someone like me who had only taught children but had no leadership experience outside the classroom be expected to know what to do as a Head Start director? My job experience had not included balancing budgets of a large program while accountants looked over my shoulder, following federal mandates and human resources policies, and dealing with teachers from 14 different centers with hundreds of children and parents involved. I look back now and wonder what gave me the courage to try. It must have been the "spunk" I was told I had.

My first day included meetings with the Federal Projects director, a social worker, a parent educator, a nurse, and some of the head teachers from the various centers. We met in scruffy old Dante School, which was built by employees of the Works Progress Administration back in the 1930s. Dante School housed the offices of the Head Start Program for Knox County Schools.

I looked young for my age, and the short skirt I wore did not help, either. But that day I felt too young. Few I was supposed to supervise were even close to my age, and my experiences were not near theirs in time and responsibilities. "What made me think I could handle this new job?" I asked myself. Then my champion arrived just in time. She supervised all the early education programs for the school system, including Head Start. When Willa Selvy walked in, people migrated to her, chatted a few minutes, and found their seats. She introduced me as her number one choice for the position of director of Knox County Schools Head Start. She said she made her selection based on the recommendation of one of the professors at the university.

Ms. Selvy did not look at me and say, "You're in charge." What she said to the audience of employees was, "She's in charge." Her endorsement carried weight and the clear expectation that others would follow my lead. Many years later I used that same expression when introducing new leaders to their expected followers.

Being in charge meant I needed to know a lot more about Head Start and a great deal more about the people who reported to me, including their job descriptions and performances. I had no problem relating to the children and their families. However, knowing all of the Head Start staff and their roles was new to me. To succeed as director, I had to be a fast learner and ask lots of questions. Doing so proved to be the key to making it through the first days on the job. My practice of asking a lot of questions instilled a sense of confidence in my direct reports that they could work with me and that I could handle the job. I wasn't a "know-it-all," who had just gotten a master's degree. Instead, I was a curious person who asked good questions of the employees and listened to their explanations and concerns.

Eventually, our Head Start Program was recognized for great gains in children's learning through innovative curricula and

As you assume new responsibilities or move into new areas, don't be afraid to ask questions. You cannot succeed pretending to know things. On the other hand, inviting people, especially employees, to share their knowledge and understanding helps form bonds as well as increases your knowledge.

parent involvement projects. We received grants for building partnerships with East Tennessee Children's Hospital. One particularly innovative Head Start program addressed the needs of children with spinal bifida. These special-needs kids were mentally able to participate in preschool programs, but their physical challenges were significant. At Head Start, I found it invigorating and fulfilling to lead the interdisciplinary teams of teachers, social workers, parents, doctors, nurses, and physical therapists who ensured that the children with spinal bifida got a Head Start education. Working with special needs children and their families was an interest of mine throughout my career.

The core team of our Head Start director's office included four staff members and me. We faced some difficult budget issues, center break-ins, and even the removal of children from homes where they had been abused. Heartbreaking concerns about children's safety weighed on me. Wondering if the children would have food over the holidays clouded many of my own holidays. After being aware of constant family dramas and hearing the parents' stories about what the families endured, I became so concerned about young children and their families that their concerns became a theme in my life.

Change in Direction: Should I Stay or Should I Study?

My Head Start administrative team wrote a successful Department of Labor grant to train teacher aides. From that experience, I realized I liked teaching adults. Thus, I made the leap from the children-only focus to children and adults. I made a critical and difficult decision to pursue a doctorate in education with a goal of becoming a professor of education. My desire was to learn more about child growth and development and more about adult learning, specifically adults who planned to become teachers. I chose curriculum and instruction in early childhood education as one of my fields of study. Almost by accident, when completing a form, I added a second field called organizational leadership.

When you determine a career path, find out the academic qualifications needed. Interview qualified individuals who are successful in that profession. Having the right qualifications is a significant key to opening doors, just as not having them can be a barrier.

Convinced that prospective teachers needed to know more about young children's cognitive, emotional, and physical growth and development, I focused on how to teach subjects effectively so that each child had rich experiences and acquired the essential knowledge and skills. But, I also wanted to make sure teachers would respect the intellectual and emotional strengths and needs of poor children and their families. I was torn between studying children and their families and actively engaging with them in the hope of making a difference in their lives. I felt like a deserter for choosing to leave the Head Start program to pursue my doctoral studies.

Leaders in publicly financed programs face many political and societal demands, as well as their own questions of whether they are doing all that can be done for those they serve. In my case, I was concerned especially about children who do not know how to express their needs and about low-income families who believed they had no voice. In Head Start, administrators lived with the challenges, pitfalls, and political demands of a publicly funded program, as well as their own concerns.

After much soul-searching, I left Head Start and gained admission to the doctoral program in education at the University of Tennessee. From my doctoral studies and my research, I learned more about children and families, as well as about administration and supervision in various organizations. I discovered a whole body of knowledge in organizational leadership. After years of leading by intuition, trial and error, and second-guessing, I learned principles of leadership, characteristics of high-performing organizations, and effective communication strategies. My studies and reflections on my experiences as a Head Start director helped form a foundation for my career path ahead.

Dedicated professors called me to task and challenged my thinking about the best ways to lead and my belief system about the dynamics of group interactions. Gifted organizers and managers from the nonprofit world and corporate life expanded my views of how groups organize themselves to be effective. Data collectors and statisticians helped me analyze probabilities and become more data-driven in decision-making. However, the faces and lives of the Head Start children never left my heart and remained close in my thinking.

While enrolled in a difficult statistics course taught by Dr. W.W. Wyatt, I derived another benefit. I met Rebecca Isbell, a graduate student with a background in early education. She and I have stayed in touch as best friends and professional colleagues over the years.

The value of a trusted professional colleague cannot be overestimated. If you are fortunate enough to develop such relationships, maintain them. Over time, the mutual benefits to you and your colleagues can be significant.

Certainly, the statistics course helped me learn more about measuring a program's progress, but the friendship of a colleague with similar interests proved to outweigh every statistical formula. Everyone in a career needs someone to be an intellectual companion, a truth reflector, a friend when the times are good, and a confidante when things are bad.

Although my intention to learn about organizational leadership as part of my doctoral studies was a fortunate afterthought, my deep interest in children, families, and education never wavered. My dissertation research on children's language development, particularly teaching them to be listening-thinkers, took an intriguing turn. I learned more about effective communication and active listening in general. These skills proved to be essential to me in resolving several dilemmas that lay ahead.

Chapter 3

A CRISIS IN LEADERSHIP

After earning my doctorate in education, I accepted a position as assistant professor on the faculty of a prominent university in another state. A little over a year after my arrival, I was asked to chair the department. The following "case," purposefully written without names, is presented in interview form as a recollection. I may have recalled it accurately, but it is not the total picture. The case relates to my first leadership dilemma in higher education. The questions that form the case were derived from telling the story to students in a leadership development training session.

CASE: ASSISTANT PROFESSOR BECOMES DEPARTMENT CHAIR

Question: Why would an assistant professor, the newest on faculty and with the lowest rank, be asked to chair the department? The equivalent in other industries would be to ask the newest employee with the lowest rank to lead a team of seasoned veterans.

Answer: When the lowest in rank and tenure is asked to chair the department, it means one thing – everyone else has turned the job down.

Question: Why did everyone else turn it down?

Answer: It was a relatively small department of about 12 people. Two of the full professors, the usual choices to chair departments, had stepped down. One professor had health problems, and the other relinquished the post because of strife in the group. Others were simply unwilling to take on the role.

Question: What were the dynamics of the department that made no one want to serve as department chair?

Answer: The dynamics can best be described as pressured, distrustful, and contentious. Think of it as a small team working with hundreds of students, equivalent to customers in business, with productivity measured in numbers of student credit hours recorded, degrees earned, papers published, and applications filed by graduate students seeking to study with star professors.

One faculty member was extremely gossipy and talkative in meetings, in hallways, and in people's offices. She questioned the merits of the department's work, charged favoritism in people's schedules, criticized the quality of some professors' teaching, and even gossiped about the personal lives of officials in the college.

Faculty meetings either were contentious or few spoke on any issue. Many found excuses for doctors' appointments on faculty meeting days.

Question: Why would you accept the position no one wanted?

Answer: My division head, the person over the department, asked me to take the position. I was naïve, full of new organizational knowledge, and eager to make a good impression in my first full-time university position. In addition, I was untenured. Non-tenured people do not turn down the division head's requests. Besides that, people there seemed to like me, and I thought I got along well with everybody, even the gossipy one. Individuals talked freely with me outside of the faculty meeting. I thought I could persuade them to communicate together as a group.

Question: What did the division head tell the department staff when you were appointed?

Answer: My appointment was disclosed in a brief memorandum, not in a department meeting, public announcement, news release, or endorsement. I had previous administrative experience, so I expected to be endorsed as someone who would be a good department chair. I suppose it was not needed. Everyone, but me, knew that the qualified leaders had turned down the position. The division head's announcement was as brief as his parting directions to me were, "Meet with all of the faculty members individually and get them to agree to work in harmony."

More Questions: Where did you begin? Whom did you meet with first? What did you say?

Answer: Nervously, I scheduled sessions with individuals throughout my first day on the job in my new office. At one time, the office was occupied by Gossipy. I started the day with her, thinking she was my biggest problem. I wanted to get her session out of the way as soon as possible.

We sat in front of the desk, not behind it, and shared social conversation. Using what I thought was my best communication techniques, I asked her thoughts about the unproductive faculty meetings.

Rather than taking my lead, she began to gossip about and criticize each of the department members. I defended each person she maligned, contradicting every statement of derision with a positive comment. Then she began talking about the "star" professor whom students were flocking to study with and whom others sought for consultations. The star professor had chaired the search committee that selected me to join the faculty. I felt positively toward him, and apparently, he had good judgement. He recommended they hire me. He was the reason I was on the faculty. (Later, we were married, indicating I had a strong and lasting attraction to him, which she did not know.)

She and I became argumentative, and our voices rose. I was no longer countering the derisive comments with positive ones; we were arguing so loudly I had to close the door. Finally, after several back-and-forth exchanges, I jumped up from my chair, opened the door and left the office with Gossipy still sitting there. Halfway down the hall to where my old office had been, I realized I had just walked out of my own new office. This scene illustrated one of my major communication and emotional failures, especially for someone who thought she could lead people to work together.

Question: What happened next? How did you remedy the situation?

Answer: When I realized I had walked out of my own office, I took a deep breath, returned, and apologized. Immediately, I asked her to come back after lunch, and I promptly canceled all the remaining meetings scheduled that day with the other faculty members. I needed time to collect my thoughts, refocus on what I was trying to accomplish in the meeting, and rethink how to approach her.

After lunch, we tentatively started our meeting over. I sincerely apologized for getting angry and for letting my emotions and nervousness bring me to a heightened state of agitation. I even apologized for leaving her in my office. I asked her if she had ever left someone in her office in error. She said no.

Acknowledging that I knew I had been the last choice of the faculty, I asked her to help me. I praised her long history of success, pointed out some specifics of her many accomplishments, and asked for her cooperation. Eventually, we discussed ways that the department faculty could function better so that our department would be viewed as productive, not dysfunctional.

Over my remaining years there, we did not become friends, but we were not enemies. We managed to have a civil, polite, and mostly productive relationship. Interestingly, as news of my confrontation with her spread, my reconciliation and consultation with the most difficult professor gained me respect from the other faculty members. Apparently, the department had more than one gossipy faculty member.

ADDITIONAL NOTES

Several times in my career, I was the youngest university professor, least in rank and title. Those experiences taught me to respect older professionals, work on improving communication, recognize my limitations, and view problems from others' perspectives. Most importantly, I learned how opportunity is not always some grand door opening; it may simply be the willingness to say, "Yes, I'll take the job," when others have turned down the position.

Sometimes agreeing to accept a responsibility that no one else wants but that is essential to the organization can help you develop new skills and demonstrate your merit as a leader. Some difficult lessons are valuable to your career.

Chapter 4

MOVING ON AND
MOVING UP

At a pivotal point during my career, a friend asked me, "Aren't you supposed to make vertical moves, not horizontal ones?" The question caused me to examine my career path, and still, I applied for what could be perceived as a lateral move.

Many women leaders tell similar stories of waiting to be tapped for roles of leadership without volunteering or applying. I did not volunteer or ask for the department chair jobs but served as department chair in two different universities. When I considered making a career move to still a third university, I resolved to actually apply for a position of department chair, a horizontal move, but one

Plan your future. And go for it. Consider what you want in life and what it will take to get you there. Don't just wait and see what comes your way. If you wait to be tapped for leadership jobs, they may not come your way.

where I took the risk and applied.

The case below is written about my experience of applying for and being selected as a department chair in a third university.

CASE: SHAKE THE DUST FROM YOUR SANDALS AND MOVE ON

A rapidly expanding university needed a department chair for a large department, and I applied and accepted the challenges. A large contingency of faculty members taught on the main campus, and small groups were stationed at four branch campuses. As might be expected, there were major communication and status problems among the faculty members.

The supervisor to whom I reported was an inspirational leader who provided sage advice and creative solutions to problems. He had a charismatic personality, a great sense of humor, and a national reputation. I was thrilled to apply for and win appointment as chair of a department under his leadership.

Unfortunately, two years later, the person who hired me retired. His successor was not kind to me, perhaps because I was the only woman department chair in the college. My interactions with him were met with chauvinistic comments, sarcasm, and embarrassing treatment. After a year of trying to improve the situation, I faced another dilemma.

Should I report his behavior to the central administration level? Should I invite a peer department chair to go with me and confront him with my concerns about how he had been treating me? Should I report him to the human resources professionals and request some specific training for him? Later, in a private conference with him, after telling him how I felt, I asked him to explain his unwanted comments and behavior toward me. He said, paraphrasing, "You are the typical softy female administrator who can't take a joke or criticism. If you can't take the heat, you should consider returning to teaching and give up administrative work."

For months I wrestled with this question: should I stay or go? With a trusted friend, I compared the pros and cons of the situation. The reasons for staying were the university's great faculty, enrollment growth, and the recent improvements in communication across campuses. In addition, my family had moved to the city from several states away. We liked the area and wanted to stay there indefinitely. But for me, the predominant cons were the humiliation, embarrassment, and lack of respect I felt because of the words, tone, and behavior of my supervisor.

My Decision to Move

An old lesson that Mother taught in Sunday school guided my decision. In Mark 6:11, (New International Version), Jesus says, "And if any place will not welcome you or listen to you, leave that place and shake the dust off your feet as a testimony against them." I decided to shake the dust from my sandals and search for a new position, leaving behind a city we thought would be our permanent home.

My father even asked me, "Shirley, why are you moving again? I'm worried about you. Can't you keep a job?" I asked Bob, my husband, to search *The Chronicle of Higher Education* and find another department head position for which I could apply.

Bob found an announcement for the opening of dean of the College of Education at the University of Kentucky. He had to convince me to apply because I thought department chair was the highest leadership level I could attain in my career. I had become an effective administrator of two departments, in jobs for which I had not applied. And, despite the supervisor's demeaning treatment, I had been successful at leading a very large department at a third university. Success in three locations must mean that department chair in higher education was the managerial position I was meant to hold. But Bob convinced me to take a chance and apply for the dean's position. Another

Change often means moving. Decide the change you want. Do not stay with a difficult supervisor, if you can possibly avoid it.

factor was that my son was in Oak Ridge, Tennessee, about 150 miles away from Lexington and would move there to attend college.

At this juncture in my career, I began to envision what I wanted to do and moved decisively toward my goal. The change drastically altered my future.

Chapter 5

BE YOURSELF,
YOUR BEST SELF

Amazed that my application for dean of the College of Education at the University of Kentucky made it through the search process, I learned as much as possible about the university and the college. Although thrilled when I was asked to interview for the position, I also was plagued with old doubts.

"Who are you, a country girl from a farm in Tennessee, applying for a position of authority in this great university? What do you know? You've never been a dean. What makes you think you can do this job?" The old adage, "Be yourself," as in William Shakespeare's "To thine own self be true," proved to be the answer to my internal questions and doubts. Also, in the back of my mind, I heard Mother's ringing voice saying, "Of course, you can," as a response to any self-doubt.

Knowing I could stay in my current position because I was not being fired helped me in the interview. It's always wise to secure a new job before leaving your old one. My experience with the "troublesome supervisor" inadvertently helped, but I did not divulge information about my discomfort with him in the interviews. Instead, I focused on my desire to find a position in which I could be more like the charismatic leader I had admired. I wanted to be at a place with high expectations, where I could encourage creativity and innovation. An added benefit was that Lexington also is a beautiful place to live. Again, I was looking for a permanent home for Bob, Brian, and me.

Remembering my other moves to Head Start director and three different department chair positions that had tested my courage helped me overcome the self-doubts. I liked the people at UK and could see myself working well with them. One of my strengths is the genuine positive regard I feel for most people. Being respected as the leader by

Have confidence in yourself. Remember what got you to this point on your career journey. Consider the winning characteristics you have developed. Recall all of those experiences and characteristics to take the next step, confidently. Be yourself, your best self.

most followers is essential to the success of the leader and the group. The chancellor took a leap of faith when he offered me the position because I had not been a dean before. I knew I had to earn the trust of the faculty and other staff as well as the chancellor to whom I was to report. I also knew the key to success in a new job is to follow the frequently heard advice, "Be yourself, your best self."

The courage to be oneself seems easy, but we often think we have to know the latest and be the greatest in terms of past accomplishments. In reality, we have to be the person who knows enough but is willing to learn more. We do not have to be the greatest, but in higher education, we have to know how to support the great thinkers and researchers, the people who do know a lot about their fields and professions. We do not need to have accomplished more than anyone else applying for the position, but we must have a track record that suggests we have what it takes to learn and handle a job at the next highest administrative level. The person responsible for making the selection must have reasons to trust that the applicant who is chosen can accomplish whatever the position demands.

In the deanship interviews, I needed courage to be myself. I bolstered my courage by telling stories of problems my team and I tackled in my previous position. One of the quotes about courage that meant a great deal to me is from Eleanor Roosevelt: "You gain strength, courage, and confidence by every experience in which you really stop to look fear in the face. You must do the thing you think you cannot do." I was fearful, but I was more excited about the prospects of the position. To grow as a leader, I was willing to leave my comfort zone.

By restraining the self-doubts, reaching deep for the courage to proceed, and relishing the adventure of being in a new place, I enjoyed the interview. It led to my appointment as dean of the College of Education at the University of Kentucky, the first woman to hold that position. One would expect that at least several women would have been appointed deans of colleges of education by the end of the 20th century because the majority of elementary and secondary school teachers are women. However, no woman had been selected at UK. Interestingly, two former male deans remained on the faculty, and two others were still living in Lexington. Not lacking for advice from former deans, I learned some valuable leadership lessons about how to work with and appreciate those who had previously held my position. These experiences served me well in later posts.

My first three years at UK can be described as a whirlwind of activity. The responsibilities of a dean and of a department chair are quite different. As dean, I was expected to interact with senior university administrators, meet with other deans on the chancellor's cabinet, work with faculty on program development, and make sure the enrollment, personnel, and finances met university and accreditation requirements. The demands of managing the relationships of our various constituencies – students, alumni, donors, public school partners, and members of the Kentucky General Assembly – did not seem like difficult tasks for me because I enjoyed interacting professionally and socially with all of the groups. However, interacting well with a variety of people does not mean everything went smoothly in my new position. Presented below in the two cases are my recollections of two of the multifaceted situations.

CASE #1: CHANGING THE CULTURE - "WE SELECTED YOU AND WE WANT YOU TO SUCCEED"

One of the first problems my assistant deans and I identified was that the College of Education faculty members were promoted and tenured at the lowest rates among the colleges of the university. The three-tiered approach of approval was made by the committees from the department, then the college, and finally the university committee. Our desire to increase the rates for promotion and tenure was a daunting task. Understanding the regulations and culture surrounding the promotion and tenure process was the first key to resolving the dilemma. We had a large number of untenured assistant professors wanting to be promoted to associate professors, but we were doubtful that some would ever make it. We also had a smaller number of discouraged associate professors who had given up trying to be promoted to full professors.

Boosting the promotion and tenure rates was not easy, but we accomplished it through the establishment of a mentoring process for the assistant professors. The culture in many colleges at the university was that assistant professors are on their own to win promotions, causing them fear and trepidation. If they were not promoted by their sixth year, their contracts were not renewed. Assistant professors often avoided speaking up in faculty meetings for fear that a senior faculty member would not agree with them and would vote to deny them promotion and tenure.

Although we lacked control over the university's rules for tenure and promotion, we did have control of the selection of people to fill the vacancies in our college, which eventually improved the promotion rate. We turned our selection process on its ear by telling potential recruits: "If we select you, we want you to succeed." We spent much more time recruiting, screening, and interviewing applicants. I was involved in interviewing candidates for all vacancies, no matter the department. When a person was selected and appointed, we celebrated the occasion by sending out announcements to professional journals in their fields, to local media in their hometowns, and to their former professors. We made it a story of prestige that this applicant had been selected to teach, conduct research, and serve in our college.

We asked the search committee chairs who helped recruit the newly employed faculty members to serve as temporary mentors. By the end of the first semester, the new faculty members each selected a permanent mentor and met with their department chair, mentor, and me. We asked them to identify their strengths, describe what they would be working on for the next year, and tell us how we could assist them because "we had selected them and we wanted them to succeed."

As an aside, many people in the process had a hard time acknowledging their strengths and preferred talking about their shortcomings and the actions they were taking to improve. After each meeting in my office with the assistant professor, mentor, and department chair, I asked the assistant professor to write up the meeting, beginning with a statement of his or her strengths. If the strengths identified at the meeting were not included, I asked the assistant professor to rewrite the report.

We are so accustomed in school and higher education to being criticized that we fail to take into account our strengths. Interestingly, the women assistant professors had more difficulty than the men in stating their strengths.

The number of meetings was a significant time commitment for me. The challenge was to keep the sessions fresh and convince the department chairs that championing the untenured faculty members was one of their roles. My team had to persuade the mentors to function as real mentors. For the senior faculty members, I rated them highly in their evaluations if they were mentoring junior faculty. At my individual meetings with department chairs, we routinely discussed the progress of the assistant professors and their involvement in contributing solutions to department problems.

At the end of the third year, we helped untenured assistant professors identify any loopholes in their plans that should be filled to enable their accomplishments to be reviewed positively in their fifth year. Such a review increased the probability that an assistant professor would be elevated to the associate professor rank and retained in the sixth year. We kept reiterating to them that "we selected you and we want you to succeed."

We marshaled the university's resources and asked members of the university-level promotion and tenure committee to make presentations to the untenured faculty. The committee members provided redacted documents, including tenure and promotion papers of people who had been successful and those who were not successful. The involvement of the university committee members sent a message to the university-wide promotion and tenure committee that we expected our untenured faculty members to be successful when they came up for review.

> *If another division of your organization is hindering your employees or your team members' advancement, as the leader, it is your responsibility to resolve the problems. Seek ways to get the decision-makers to see the value of your team members.*

We dramatically improved the college's success rate for promoting assistant professors to associate professors with tenure, as well as increasing their salaries. However, we were less successful in promoting associate professors to full professors. After faculty members are tenured, they have no time limit for applying for a full professorship. I knew that we had some associate professors already performing at levels higher than those of some of their full professor counterparts. However, the rigor of constructing a dossier, the fear of criticism, and the desire not to have additional demands kept many from applying.

When a few associate professors became full professors, we celebrated their successes elaborately by having dinners and parties for them, inviting their families to a college meeting, and announcing their accomplishments by whatever professional means they wanted, such as through announcements in journals and mailings to their professional associations. Interestingly, what they enjoyed the most was the invitations to their families to be a part of the celebrations.

CELEBRATING SUCCESS FOR STAFF - A "MUGGING"

Measuring success and planning celebrations for faculty members were relatively easy tasks. However, when faculty members were not successful, it took an emotional toll on the person, their families, colleagues, and me. It is extremely difficult to evaluate people whom we value as people, but whose productivity for the organization is questionable.

We had a great deal of information about assistant and associate professors, such as ratings by students, critical evaluations of their research and publications, and letters of recommendation about their service from partners in the schools or other agencies. Once achieved, our celebrations of promotion and tenure were noteworthy because we recognized the tremendous amount of work they had accomplished and had documented in their dossiers with support letters and positive critiques of their publications and service records.

While we had a great deal of performance information about faculty members, we knew far less about staff members who served in support roles, such as secretaries, executive assistants, information technology professionals, accountants, and grants managers. However, everyone in the college had experienced their services, so my administrative team and I became good listeners to assess accurately the job performances of the staff. In addition, their supervisors noted which ones had the "going beyond" attitude.

Take every opportunity to celebrate the successes of your colleagues and employees in the organization. Do it joyously and with enthusiasm.

The idea of "mugging" people was to unexpectedly present a coffee mug bearing our college insignia to the person who demonstrated "going beyond" what was required. We presented the mugs during a college-wide meeting. It became a way of acknowledging a staff member who consistently performed at a high level or someone who went beyond what was expected to help meet an unusual need. Interestingly, when I went back years later to the college for a visit, many of the people still had their coffee mugs from the "mugging ceremony" in special places on their bookshelves.

What we did not accomplish was to celebrate team efforts more effectively. We started recognizing teams in the college meetings and presenting each member with a mug, but the "mugging" idea belonged to individual efforts. We needed another recognition idea for teams.

Suffice it to say, the relationships, the people, and problem-solving parts of my position as dean were what I relished. Our faculty and staff were generally very productive, eager to take on challenges, and pleased that their efforts were acknowledged, not just in an evaluation for a file or a promotion to win a higher rank or pay raise, but in public recognition.

CASE #2: "WHO DO YOU THINK YOU ARE, SUPERWOMAN? TWO JOBS SIMULTANEOUSLY?"

After three years as dean, the chancellor unexpectedly offered me a different position within the university. I was stunned by the offer and torn about accepting. Leave the job I loved, with our turn-around story on faculty promotion and tenure and with our good relationships with faculty, with my superior leadership team, and the quality support staff throughout the college?

The university had created the new position of Vice Chancellor for Academic Services, to which the following offices and functions reported: Dean of Undergraduate Studies, Admissions, Registrar, Enrollment Management, Assessment and Institutional Data, Teaching and Learning Center, Honors Program, Merit Scholarship Office, and Athletic Academics.

I was very hesitant to step away from my college to take on many of the central roles of the university. After meeting several times with the chancellor, I offered a compromise. I asked for these changes: 1. Promote the two assistant deans in my office to associate deans and assign some additional duties to them; 2. Permit me to continue to work with the College of Education in the morning; and 3. Allow me to work on my new assignment as vice-chancellor for Academic Services every afternoon.

Actually, I did not expect the president of the system or the chancellor of the campus to accept my compromise, but they did. Therefore, for the next three years, I "worked" two jobs simultaneously. Frankly, it was only because of the caliber of each of the directors of these offices and my own College of Education associate deans, Rob Shapiro and Rosetta Sandidge, key assistants Rosemary Waters and Mary Ann Vimont, and the department chairs that I was able to do both jobs simultaneously. My administrative assistants in the dean's office and in the vice chancellor's office orchestrated the schedules and duties to be sure I met my commitments fairly to each unit. I was grateful that people in the College of Education did not want me to leave and that people reporting to me in the Academic Services office wanted to work with me. Only one senior professor said I was not being fair to my first job of dean, asking me if I had a superwoman complex and still had to prove myself. Perhaps it was not a superwoman complex, but rather a little country girl still trying to prove herself.

Colleagues from around the country questioned my judgment, and my husband and other family members thought I was being taken advantage of. However, the extraordinary experiences I encountered in two different jobs prepared me for the wide range of responsibilities I would need for my next position. The beneficial responsibilities added to my resume. Additionally, I observed firsthand the roles the chancellor of the campus and the president of the system played and the scope of their circles of leadership, including interacting with elected officials, donors, alumni, athletics, as well as traversing the campus politics.

The time may come for you to move on, to take your expertise and experience to meet a new challenge. Remember the people you leave behind and keep in touch, especially with key staff. Provide references for them and support them when they are ready for new positions. They deserve that. But embrace the future and the new people without regret or reservation. They deserve that.

Even with all of these new and exciting challenges and access to a broad spectrum of university life, I was planning to ask the chancellor to name someone else for the vice chancellor post and let me return to the dean's position full-time. Before I could place that request in writing, another opportunity, which is described in the next chapter, profoundly changed my life forever.

Chapter 6

WHAT ARE THE CHANCES?

For career moves, leaders rely on references from their past employers, present colleagues, and often are advised to expand their networks of professional friends. Bob Beaudine in his book, *The Power of Who,* challenges leaders to recognize their existing network of supporters. "You already know someone right now who knows the person who will help you achieve your goal or hire you or introduce you to the person you need to meet."

Frank Dickey, the former president of the University of Kentucky, was the "who" in my life who helped me to envision and eventually realize a new goal. He also was a previous dean of the College of Education and became a friend and colleague during my six years there. Active in the college, university and community activities, Dr. Dickey used his connections to introduce me to state and locally elected officials and school system leaders. He and our spouses also enjoyed the horse races at Keeneland, and we visited some beautiful horse farms. In the process, he also introduced me to some prominent philanthropists.

When the president of the University of Kentucky decided to retire, my name was on a long list mentioned for the presidency. From my awareness of the Kentucky governor's admiration for one candidate and conversations with some trustees, I was certain I would not be considered. As is true of many state universities, the governor also served as chair of the board.

Fortunately, Lee Todd, a former UK engineering professor and successful technology entrepreneur, was selected. Lee was highly devoted to students from the State of Kentucky and to advancements in science, engineering, and technology. I had gotten to know him and felt he was the right choice. Lee asked me to consider becoming a part of his administration's leadership team, and I was considering it when another opportunity for me surfaced. Again, Dr. Dickey was instrumental in opening a door for me.

While my husband Bob and I thought we had found our forever home in beautiful Lexington, Kentucky, the emotional pull for me to return home to Tennessee also was present. My parents were elderly and in declining health. Their needs made me ask some soul-searching questions, particularly after a few emergency drives of more than six hours to be with them. I also felt an obligation and gratitude to my home State of Tennessee for my public education from elementary through graduate school, for my scholarships, and for those public school teachers and professors who believed in me enough to encourage me.

In discussions with Dr. Dickey, I expressed concern about living so far from my parents and my desire to give back to public education in my own state. I asked him if he would write a reference for me for a deanship or other university post if I could find something in Tennessee nearer my parents. He surprised me by saying, "No." Stunned, I began thanking him for supporting me through my years at UK. Then he said, "I think it is time you consider being a president." He had seen an announcement of an opening for the president of the University of Memphis, just 72 miles from my parents' farm where I grew up.

My first reaction was that "they will never appoint a woman president at the University of Memphis." Bob, who had been highly supportive of my previous career moves, told me I was wasting my time. After some real soul-searching, reading about the University of Memphis, and asking a lot of professional colleagues about the university, I decided to allow my name to be placed in nomination.

The nomination process is used for the highest-level administrative positions in universities. Dr. Frank Dickey nominated me to the search firm and Dr. Charles Manning, Chancellor of the Tennessee Board of Regents system. I am omitting many other steps in the process, but some steps are worth delineating because they explain how key influence makers become a part of a leader's life.

FROM INTERVIEWS TO SELECTION OF A PRESIDENT

Quite different from the searches by headhunters for CEOs in the business world, the search for a university president often takes a year. Search firms work with a search committee, hold multiple meetings, arrange for interviews, and usually survey various constituencies about the types of candidates they think are appropriate. Dr. Charles Manning, chancellor of the Tennessee Board of Regents, a recent appointee of Governor Don Sundquist, was embarking on his first university president search process in Tennessee.

The search committee for the president of the University of Memphis position was bifurcated, with some members appointed by Chancellor Manning, and others by the Board of Visitors, an influential group of business and community leaders from Memphis. No other university in the state of Tennessee had a Board of Visitors and a governing board. Governor Sundquist served as the chair of the Board of Regents and appointed each regent, who represented geographic areas of the state. He charged Chancellor Manning with establishing a search committee. The Board of Visitors, appointed by the board chairman, Dr. Willard Sparks, also appointed people to the search committee. Dr. Sparks decided he would serve on the search committee, as well. If this process seems complicated, it was.

Knowing the selection process for the president was a lengthy one, I had not told my mother and father about being nominated. I did not want them to get their hopes up that I would be moving closer to them. However, unbeknown to me, my name appeared on a list of finalists published in *The Commercial Appeal,* the Memphis newspaper. Of course, my parents called me right away after many people in my hometown contacted them. Knowing the search process was an arduous one and fraught with many possible upsets along the way, I discouraged them from thinking I would actually get the position and even used the comment I had heard earlier, "They will never select a woman as president of the University of Memphis."

I was the only woman on the list, which also had one minority male. At least one woman and at least one minority on a list of candidates are often requirements before search firms have their lists approved to continue the process. However, undaunted, I thought, "What do I have to lose? It is an honor to be in the top ten and just being on the list has already given my parents a thrill." But, in reality, I really wanted the job, not just for my parents, but for the challenge and excitement.

As a dean and a vice chancellor at the University of Kentucky, I observed closely the situations, issues, and dilemmas the chancellor of the campus and the president of the system faced. (Note: In Kentucky, the system head is called president and the campus head is called chancellor. For the Tennessee Board of Regents, it is the opposite.)

I found myself analyzing how I would handle the same situations a chancellor or the president faces if I were in charge. Therefore, when Dr. Dickey nominated me, I was ready to describe how I would prioritize and approach current issues that I knew faced the University of Memphis. If I were being considered as a serious candidate for the job, I would be asked a series of "what would you do questions" about those topics.

KNOW THE SEARCH PROCESS, THE COMMITTEE, THE COMPETITORS, AND THE CONTEXT BEFORE THE INTERVIEW

Airport hotel interviews were scheduled for the ten finalists. Each had to fly to an airport and meet with the search committee on neutral territory. Before my interview, I had done my own reconnaissance. Of course, I checked out the other finalists' credentials and had to fight the old self-doubts when I realized sitting presidents were on the interview list. Naturally, I reviewed the list of search committee members and tried to think of their interests by virtue of the positions they held.

Don't blow your interview. You won't get all the opportunities you think you deserve. Unfortunately, that is especially true if you are a woman. When opportunity knocks, be prepared to answer resoundingly with everything you need to be successful. Whatever opportunity you are pursuing, do your homework.

The most telling part of my preparation occurred during my anonymous visit to the campus. No one knew me at that time. My name was on a list, but my photograph was not published. I walked in and out of every building on the main campus, observed how people greeted me in offices when I asked for directions, saw physical plant people around the campus, watched students interacting, and hung out at the university center.

At one point before the airport interview, I almost backed out. Even though the University of Memphis campus was in a beautiful part of town, I was overwhelmed by the amount of attention the physical buildings and grounds needed, not one of my areas of experience or expertise.

What convinced me to stay in the search was the information I read about the faculty, signature programs, and a deeply held belief that every public urban university should be connected to the events of the city. That and the fact that I had long had a love affair with Memphis. Growing up in West Tennessee, it had been my New York. Memphis was the place where we shopped for school clothes when our cotton crop was good enough. It was the site of the Pink Palace Museum, where I saw my first original art show, and the Mid-South Fair. My high school class saw famous performers there, including Elvis Presley. In Memphis, I enjoyed seeing the movie *Cleopatra* in a historic theater. On special occasions, our family went to the zoo and had picnics in Audubon Park. None of the other candidates had this deep attraction to Memphis.

However, I had been away from the Memphis area for more than 35 years. Times had changed. Martin Luther King's tragic assassination in Memphis had caused outsiders to have a dismal perception of the city. Yet, on the positive side, Memphis leaders established the

National Civil Rights Museum at the Lorraine Motel on the very site where Dr. King was shot.

With the University of Memphis named for the city where I always wanted to live, having a job that involved the city took on even more meaning for me. Of course, working at the university also meant I could be near my elderly parents.

I started reading the *The Commercial Appeal* daily and learned that racial tensions still permeated local politics and the City Council. Mayor Willie Herenton, an African-American former school superintendent, was elected for four terms, or 16 years. Mayor Herenton drove much of the political debate, and the Fords, another prominent African-American family, had a powerful long-standing influence. Ford family members held numerous elected offices, including Harold Ford, Sr., and later Harold Ford, Jr., in the U.S. Congress. I wondered whether or not they could accept a white women as president, primarily because an African-American also was on the top ten list.

Even though I had grown up in a racially mixed community and had minority students and families in my classrooms, in Head Start, and in my university life on several campuses, often candidates are judged by their most recent experience. At the time, the University of Kentucky had a student population of about nine percent African-Americans, far less than the one-third at that time on the University of Memphis campus. Lexington had significantly fewer minority citizens than Memphis and Shelby County. At that time, the population was almost evenly divided between African-Americans and whites.

From several African-American colleagues at UK, I asked for advice and information about the University of Memphis and the Memphis community. I was encouraged by Dr. Sharon Porter Robinson, a prominent African-American alum and executive at a national education association; Lauretta Byars, vice chancellor for Minority Affairs; Retia Scott Walker, dean of the College of Human Environmental Sciences; and John Harris, former dean of the College of Education. Their encouragement was tempered by their feelings that Memphis would be more of a challenge with race relations than I encountered at UK in Lexington, Kentucky. Nonetheless, their sentiments were, "Go for it!" and I was grateful when they said, "Use our names as references."

Dr. Robinson knew Maxine Smith, a well-known civil rights advocate and former secretary of the NAACP, who was on the search committee as both a member of the Board of Regents and the Board of Visitors. I asked Sharon many questions about Dr. Smith and read about her civil rights triumphs and stances. Sharon assured me that if I were selected, Dr. Smith would be a great advocate. Until in declining health, she was very supportive of the university in numerous initiatives and of me personally.

The search committee was composed of about 20 people, including a dean, student affairs administrator (who later served on my leadership team), a state legislator, and several business people who were members of the Board of Visitors. A key search committee member was Dr. Willard Sparks, the chairman of the Board of Visitors, a well-known philanthropist, economist, and the CEO of a commodity trading company. He played a pivotal role in my interview and in my early years at the university.

At the airport where the top ten candidates were gathered, the interviews were scheduled over two days. We each had individual sessions with the large search committee which included as observers Chancellor Manning and executives from the search firm. In my interview, as I was being given polite, softball questions, I thought, "They have no intention of selecting me."

Then, something spurred Dr. Sparks to ask what I would do if I could build an institute of technology, a project that had been on the books for a while but had not materialized. The meeting came to life with our question and answer exchange. People started asking me about athletics, fundraising, budget management, and leadership style – questions that I knew they would ask a candidate they were taking seriously. At the end of the session, they hurriedly stood up and shook my hand. The conversation with Dr. Sparks continued out the door and into the hallway. I firmly believe that if Willard had not asked the hard questions, I would not have been taken seriously as a candidate for president of the University of Memphis. I later learned that the two women on the search committee pushed for my consideration, as well.

Making it to the final three from the top ten was a milestone. One sitting president and one vice president remained with me on the list of the final three. The next elimination step was the two days' worth of on-campus interviews with members of the search committee, as well as separate open forum meetings with students, faculty, staff, and central administrators.

ARE YOU TOUGH ENOUGH? DO YOU KNOW ENOUGH?

Two prevalent themes surfaced in the on-campus interviews. These same questions are ones many women face in interviews for leadership positions in other professions, as well. They may be phrased differently depending on the environment, but the first is "Are you tough enough?" and the second is "Do you know enough?"

I was ready for the "Are you tough enough?" question. For example, in one of the faculty interviews, the tough enough question was phrased, "Can you fire a football coach?" My immediate reply was, "You bet your boots I can."

Of course, I went on to explain that whether the person was a coach, a scientist, a janitor, or a faculty member, if there was cause, I was tough enough to fire him or her. Little did I know that during my 12 years as president, I would be involved in troubling decisions about dismissing two football coaches. Other probing questions were asked about athletics, local politics, race relations, and the president's role as champion for the university with the Board of Regents, the governor, and other state officials in Nashville.

"Are you tough enough to stand up to challenges from these prominent and powerful people?" When the question was asked, a seemingly unrelated story popped into my mind. I told them about my experience the previous summer at the United Nations, working with the civil society organizations on education issues. I met a woman from Africa who held a school for girls under a tree because the girls were not welcomed in the village school. As president of the Association for Childhood Education International (ACEI), I had the privilege of going to the UN that summer and representing ACEI alongside other education organizations. I told the people who wondered if I was tough enough that I had a lot of experience at being tough, but also that I gain courage when I hear what really "tough" people endure.

Collectively, the woman from Africa, ACEI, and many other organizations were striving to insert language into the UN declarations that would guide ministers of education worldwide to ensure that girls receive an elementary education. I told the audience that I do not lack the will to fight, or determination, and that I try to do the right thing. If the woman from Africa can come to New York to fight for the rights of the village girls, I certainly can fight for our university and even for the children of Orange Mound, which is the poor neighborhood near the campus. Firing a football coach or any other employee for the right reasons is not a sign of toughness.

What you fight "for" is a sign of toughness.

The second probing question asked of me and usually asked of women is whether they know enough. This question often relates to knowledge about finances. Again, I had dealt with budgets and finances all my life, but they assumed I did not know enough. I anticipated the financial and budget questions. Ahead of the interview, I contacted the acting vice president for business and finance at Memphis and asked for a copy of the university's budget. Reluctant at first to provide it, he said, "There is a copy in the library," to which I replied, "I will gladly pay the cost if you will overnight it to me." He said, "No other candidate has asked for a copy of the budget." I replied that I was not like the other candidates and that I wanted to know how the university allocated its funds. He sent the budget, and I poured over it with business and finance colleagues at the University of Kentucky.

In my answers to questions from different campus groups, I let them know that I was tough enough to face the challenges and knew my way around a budget and university finances. I also mentioned that I had visited the campus previously, read about the university's programs, reviewed the strategic plan, and called esteemed colleagues around the country to ask questions about outstanding members of the Memphis faculty and about the reputations of deans.

In interviews with the vice presidents and senior directors, as well as the president's office staff, most showed interest in my leadership style and my vision for the university. Also, because the interviews took place at a time when there was considerable discussion about the national reform movement, they wished to know whether they would have to start over with yet another reform plan. On questions of leadership style, I framed my responses using my leadership philosophy shaped during my time as dean at UK. The best education leaders are "people-oriented and goal-motivated," I replied repeatedly. I also promised that the specifics for any new reform plans I might propose would not happen until we worked together for a few months.

The interviews were so exhilarating that when I left the campus, I was exhausted. However, the lingering question remained. Will these two men, heads of the Tennessee Board of Regents and the Board of Visitors, recommend a woman as President of the University of Memphis? What were the chances?

Chapter 7

WALKING IN MEMPHIS

The length of the search process from nomination to selection, the interview dynamics, the weeks of delay, and waiting for news were nerve-wracking. Convinced that they were not going to select a woman president for the University of Memphis, I went back to work at the University of Kentucky and was contemplating what I would tell President Todd if he was still interested in me for his leadership team.

However, before I could contact President Lee Tood, the Tennessee Board of Regents Chancellor Charles Manning called me in late January 2001 to offer me the position - as their unanimous choice. Later, I learned "unanimous choice" was used as a last vote to ensure solidarity on the search committee. Negotiations back and forth took a couple of days. I remember exactly where I was standing in our home in Lexington when I said, "Yes." The next day, over closed-circuit television, Chancellor Manning announced to the whole campus my appointment as the 11th president of the University of Memphis.

Incidentally, Manning announced two women presidents for the State of Tennessee on the same day. We were the first women university presidents in the Board of Regents System. The news was so unusual in 2001 that National Public Radio carried the story that Sherry Hoppe had been named president of Austin Peay State University and Shirley Raines had been named president of the University of Memphis. Since our announcements, we claimed the unusual right as the first women presidents of universities in the Tennessee Board of Regents system, but the real significance was that I was the first woman president of the University of Memphis.

Back in Lexington, while I was working in my College of Education office, the phones began ringing with calls from Dr. Sparks, Memphis news media, and the deans and vice presidents on both campuses wishing me the best. Two calls came in quite prematurely with problems for me to solve in Memphis. Parents from the Barbara K. Lipman Child Study Center requested new playground

> *Saying "no" to early requests does not make you popular, but with any leadership appointment, it is crucial to know from the start when your authority begins and how much authority you have.*

equipment. A university neighbor called to complain about students parking on her street. The callers wanted me to resolve their issues in January, and I had until July before my first official day as president. While the callers' problems and proposals were premature, they were indicators of the involvement and the responsiveness the community expected from the new university president.

In the intervening months, I asked for advice from the outgoing UK president and the chancellor, as well as a number of key administrators. They willingly gave me advice and encouragement. Some of the advice was quite specific, as related to budgets, athletics, and retention of the best faculty members. One Egyptian professor gave me a souvenir replica of King Tut's sarcophagus and advised me to "bury old ideas."

The UK Athletics Director told me that before he became director, he advised people to ignore anonymous complaints. After he became A.D., he found anonymous information could be important and should be investigated.

The president of the system told me to make friends with the governor and his staff. The chancellor of the campus told me to plan to stay five years only because I would wear out my welcome by then. Others gave advice as they recalled how they felt when a new campus administrator came on-board. I heard the advice to listen, listen, listen, over and over again, but I also heard, be yourself and let them get to know you. You are not aloof, so don't let the title go to your head.

My UK team in the dean's office and the vice chancellor's office prepared for a smooth transition. I felt prepared for my new job, but nothing could have prepared me for my first visits to Memphis to greet the campus community and the city at large.

Pyramid Arena Introduction – Women's Greetings

The City of Memphis is famous for blues, barbeque, and basketball, University of Memphis Tigers basketball and later the professional team, the Grizzlies. Shortly after the announcement of my appointment as president, I was invited to a Memphis Tigers basketball game in the iconic Pyramid. Because some of the largest crowds in Memphis assembled for basketball games, it seemed appropriate for me to be introduced to the Memphis community in the Pyramid Arena.

Bob and I watched the first half of the game from the interim president's box. At half-time, we were escorted through the fans down to the floor of the arena where we would be introduced to the crowd. The sports information director kept trying to hurry us along as we descended the steps through the fans. However, he had not anticipated what would happen.

Men often sat on the aisles, and their wives or women friends sat in the next seat over. At each step, women started leaning over their husbands and shaking my hand, saying things like, "so proud of you," "at last a woman," "way to go, sister," "I'm a graduate," "I want my daughter to meet you." Because of all of the greetings and handshakes, we were late getting down to the arena floor when the announcer jokingly said, "Just like a woman to be late." He never said that again.

At the center of the basketball court, the applause was enthusiastic and continued even after the officials and television crews were ready to start the second half of the game. As the Pep Band played the Tiger Fight Song, we waved goodbye from the arena floor and began climbing back up to the concourse level on the opposite side of the arena. From each row, the warm greetings started again. Young women, students, and elderly women, many dressed in blue school colors, reached out to me with words of encouragement and excitement.

At the concourse level, a female police officer rushed up behind me. I thought she wanted to escort us around to our box, but her purpose was to shake my hand. Then, as Bob and I walked along the concourse, women servers began coming out from the concession stands to shake my hand and express their excitement, some even saying, "I never thought they would hire a woman as president at Memphis."

The memory of my announcement at the Pyramid and all those women who just wanted to shake my hand will stay with me for the rest of my life. I knew that

In the early days of a new position, remember that people are judging you on first impressions and how you treat them. Be hospitable and genuinely interested, interesting, and interactive.

being appointed as the first woman president of the University of Memphis was monumental for me, but I had no idea the measure of meaning it held for women on campus and women and girls in the city.

MISTAKEN IDENTITY: LOOKING FOR THE PRESIDENT OF THE UNIVERSITY

Over the course of the next few months, I made several trips to Memphis. Donors with private planes generously invited me to use their planes to attend special events.

The Fogelman College of Business and Economics was preparing for an accreditation visit soon, so I scheduled to meet with them for an update about their accreditation study. Mr. Bobby Fogelman, one of the family for whom the College of Business and Economics is named and a founder of the Board of Visitors, sent a private plane to Lexington to pick me up.

The plan was for me to meet the pilots and take an immediate flight to the meeting in Memphis. I arrived early and checked in at the reception desk of the private airport for my first trip on a private jet. Groups of pilots and passengers milled around in the lounge area. I waited and waited, but no one announced a plane from Memphis. Finally, I went back to the desk and asked when the plane was expected. There was a plane from Memphis already on the ground.

My request prompted the desk attendant to go over to some pilots sitting at a round table and inquire of them about their expected passenger. I saw her point over at me, and they shook their heads, "No." She came to me and said, 'No, it is not you. They are waiting for a Dr. Raines, the new President of the University of Memphis." Showing my drivers' license to her, I said, "I'm Dr. Shirley Raines." She rushed over with my driver's license to the pilots, who jumped to attention and apologized profusely for the mistake of expecting the new president to be a man. They treated me like a queen, made up lost time on the short flight, and said they hoped I would not tell Mr. Fogelman what happened. I did not tell the story until years later.

Meeting Legends and Leaders

Several other visits to the city before my actual starting date proved to be advantageous. I met community leaders, heads of foundations and companies, as well as elected officials, people I fondly called "legends and leaders."

> *Find or create opportunities to meet leaders from government, business, education, philanthropy, and organized religion. These are the people who are the "difference-makers" in the community. Their support and advice can be extremely valuable.*

Dr. Maxine Smith, a civil rights legend in the city, had served on the search committee, representing both the Tennessee Board of Regents and the Board of Visitors. Ironically, as a young and highly qualified African-American student, Maxine Smith had been denied admission to the very university over which she now held governance authority.

From following the news in *The Commercial Appeal*, I learned Dr. Benjamin Hooks, another civil rights legend, was scheduled to address University School, a private, mostly white, school in Memphis. Bob and I traveled there to hear him speak. Dr. Hooks, a gifted orator, challenged the audience with uplifting stories and after his speech, he greeted me cordially with genuine encouragement.

Mrs. Frances Hooks, me, my husband Bob Canady, and Dr. Benjamin Hooks, legendary civil rights leader in the nation and a religious leader in the community.

Dr. and Mrs. Hooks, Bob and I became friends. I spoke at Dr. Hooks' church on Women's Day; he was one of the speakers and offered a prayer at my inauguration ceremony. He advised me on race relations and sometimes on administrative matters. I was touched deeply that even when his health was poor, he came to the funeral services for Mother, which were in a small town over 72 miles from his home in Memphis.

Rich in history and rich in problems, Memphis and the university were bound together with the desire to right many wrongs. Dr. Hooks and Dr. Smith introduced me to the African-American leader community and to leaders from many different segments of society. An endorsement from Dr. Hooks or Dr. Smith carried great weight in any community.

THE PERSON WHO INTRODUCES YOU MAKES A DIFFERENCE

Both Dr. Smith and Dr. Hooks continued to make contacts for me with political leaders in Memphis. Willard Sparks also was instrumental in making pivotal introductions with philanthropic organizations and community leaders.

Known for its generous residents, Memphis routinely ranks in the top five in giving among America's top 50 cities. In 2015, Memphians gave more than 5 percent of their income to charity. Recognizing the significance of the philanthropic community to the well-being of the university, Dr. Sparks made arrangements and accompanied me to meet the directors and founders of four of the city's major foundations.

Willard also arranged meetings with two of the city's legendary entrepreneurs, Frederick W. Smith and Kemmons Wilson, Sr. Mr. Smith is the founder, CEO, and president of FedEx Corporation, headquartered in Memphis. With more than 30,000 employees in the area, FedEx has a tremendous impact on the economy at a local level, and their influence is felt nationally and globally. Mr. Wilson was the founder of Holiday Inns and the modern franchising arrangements for hotels and motels.

Mr. Smith and the FedEx leadership team played pivotal roles in financially supporting and advising many university projects, as well as philanthropic organizations throughout the city. Fred Smith gave the address at my inauguration. On several occasions, he assisted me when I sought his advice and never failed to amaze me with his intellect, drive, and dedication.

Kemmons Wilson, Sr., and his family donated the funds for an on-campus Holiday Inn. They gave the land and helped us build, stock, staff, and manage our own hotel. We located a museum in Mr. Wilson's honor in the hotel that also housed our newly established School of Hospitality and Resort Management.

The officials of the four local foundations proved to be equally influential. The presidents and executive directors of the Assisi, Hyde Family Foundation, Plough, and the Wilson Family Foundation invested in our programs, not just our buildings. They enabled the university to advance on several fronts. As leaders, corporate executives, and people of community influence, they did not hesitate to indicate the programs and community efforts that meant the most to them. Given their success and influence, I was grateful to the foundation leaders, African- American leaders, and legendary corporate giants for their advice, counsel, and contributions.

WALKING IN MEMPHIS

"Walking in Memphis" became my theme song to symbolize my conviction that the university should be a part of Memphis, not a separate entity. A song sung often in the city and at major events, "Walking in Memphis" was written by Marc Cohen who composed the lyrics while on an actual visit to Memphis. The lyrics mention Elvis Presley's home, Graceland, Al Green's preaching, and W.C. Handy's statue. Cohen's walking on Beale Street lyrics even imagined the ghost of Elvis. The places and names in the song are known to all who have lived in and around Memphis.

The song evoked my memory of wanting to live in Memphis. I remembered my roots as the farm girl who turned her face to the sky to watch longingly as airplanes flew high above our cotton fields. Now, I felt so fortunate. I would live in Memphis, walk in Memphis, and look out of the windows of planes from Memphis at the farmland that stretched out far below.

WALKING ON THE CAMPUS

The group for whom I had the most natural affinity was the faculty because of my teaching background. I greatly valued academics and heralded our faculty's accomplishments. Yet, as I learned more about the various operating divisions, I soon realized the importance of the intricate puzzle that made the six divisions of the university function well together: Academic Affairs; Athletics; Business and Finance; Communication, Marketing and Public Relations; Technology and Information Systems; and Student Affairs.

A department in the Business and Finance Division was the physical plant. Employees of the physical plant became significant to me in the early days of being

Greet with respect all the people who reach out to you. Seek opportunities to meet others at all stations of life and job levels. Give people the opportunity to see you as a real person, not a title. Listen and learn what you can. Everyone you meet will know something that you don't know.

president. Perhaps because of my farm work background, I always related well to the people who work with their hands to make a living.

Each year, between the spring and summer semesters when most of the students and faculty were away from campus, the physical plant employees had a picnic. When I was in Memphis for a visit, I made a surprise appearance at their picnic.

Housekeepers, electricians, plumbers, food service and residence life workers, campus planners, as well as the administrators gathered on campus for a day of leisure away from their jobs. At the picnic, I witnessed huge barbeque smokers, corn hole and horseshoe competitions, performances of Memphis soul and rock music, as well as constant laughter and the swapping of stories.

While a few people made brief speeches, the employees mostly lounged in lawn chairs under the huge trees and enjoyed a day of leisure. No one knew I was coming to the picnic. I drove up in a golf cart, got out, and started shaking hands and telling people how pleased I was to meet them. I asked what he or she did for physical plant operations. They were not accustomed to having the president visit their picnic, and they certainly did not expect the new president, even before I took office, to be there. News of my visit spread and I credit that early event as setting a stage of cooperation with the physical plant division that proved productive over the years.

In the first few weeks on campus, I visited every building and obtained the names of the employees who worked in those buildings. I complimented them on their work to keep the buildings clean and well-maintained. However, I did not hesitate to ask the physical plant supervisor for plans for improvement when buildings needed more attention.

News spread of my random visits to different parts of the campus. Without workers knowing when and where I would visit, I learned the usual building conditions, rather than the temporary result of a speedy cleanup. While this type of early attention to the physical conditions of the buildings and grounds on campus may seem surprising, it was necessary because the disrepair, littering, and general appearance of the grounds did not set the right tone for recruiting or welcoming new students and faculty.

When I walked across campus, if I saw litter, I stopped and picked it up. Some administrators complained about me doing this because it made their walks across campus with me too long. Soon, the groundskeepers, students, and the physical plant employees were paying much more attention to how our University looked. I enlisted student groups to make the campus a litter-free place of pride.

Establishing the Leadership Team before Taking Office

In the interim before I took office, the most important meetings I had were with the university's leadership team, which was called the President's Council.

I promised the vice presidents and athletic director that I would not make any replacement appointments before I arrived in July. I agreed to get to know them and their operations before making personnel changes. Some university presidents ask all of their senior administrators to resign and then reapply if they want to stay in their positions. I thought the resignation-reapplication process caused too much turmoil and anxiety. Because I thought I wanted most of them to continue on my leadership team, the deliberations about people and positions could wait until I arrived in July for more sustained face to face interactions.

When I deliberated for a longer time about whether or not to retain a particular individual, his wife called me. She told me that it was important that he be appointed sooner than later. I listened politely and said I would be in touch with her husband soon. I called him, but not to confirm his appointment. Instead, I told him, "I do not expect you to call my husband and discuss university business and likewise I do not plan to discuss university business or your appointment with your wife." I doubt seriously that any man in my position would have received that call. It was couched as a woman-to-woman talk.

COMMUNICATING EARLY WITH FACULTY, STAFF, AND A FAMOUS COACH

When my first official day in office finally arrived, Bob and I were greeted by the faculty, staff, and coaches at a reception in the Administration Building. The rotunda of this beautiful, classical, columned brick building has long been the site of most campus-wide receptions. The grand staircase from the rotunda to my second-floor office was graced with the portraits of former university presidents. It was not lost on me that no portrait of a woman was among them. Bob and I walked past these portraits, descended the stairs, and received a warm welcoming round of applause.

I had prepared some brief comments. The podium and microphone had been tested and were ready for me. Except that the former president was 6'4," and all of the podiums on campus fit him. I was almost a foot shorter, and none fit me. I turned the microphone to the side and stood beside the podium. If I had stood behind it, I would have appeared as a floating head.

People poured in from every floor of the building and through all the doors to the rotunda. I was struck by the numbers, and I recognized some folks I had seen during the interview process. During the reception, I noticed a handsome, energetic man, who looked familiar. With others making a way for him, he moved near the front of the receiving line. I recognized him as John Calipari, the head coach of the Memphis Tigers basketball team. Other coaches mingled casually with the lines of people, and no one stepped aside for them, but the men's basketball coach was different. The crowd parted for him.

When I met Coach Calipari, I asked him if he knew C.M. Newton, the athletic director at UK. I mentioned that he and I worked together closely because athletic academic advising reported to me in my vice chancellor's role at UK. I casually asked about the basketball team's graduation rate. With some reluctance, he replied something to the effect that we would talk about that later. We did.

COMMUNITY INVITATIONS – WALKING IN MEMPHIS

Churches play a prominent role in Memphis society, often called the heart of the Bible-belt. Soon after my appointment as president was announced, Bob and I received invitations to visit their churches from ministers of large churches, pastors of small ones, and communities throughout the city and county. I made a stack of the letters as they arrived, and one by one, for most of the first year, Bob and I showed up at churches throughout the city. We visited African-American, white, Protestant, and Catholic churches. The visits to churches helped us get to know our fellow citizens, other than the people of the academic community, prominent executives, and philanthropists. During these church visits "Walking in Memphis" took on new significance.

In our second year at the university, Bob and I joined Christ United Methodist Church near our home. We went to the worship service regularly; however, I found it difficult to be a part of Sunday school classes because people turned to me for opinions too often. People used that time to tell me what the university should or should not be doing, particularly in athletics. I never quite navigated the "staying in the background mode" I needed for time away from the university.

First Man, Husband

Because I was the first woman president of the university, initially people wanted to know what to do with Bob. The wives of university presidents are often called "First Ladies of the University." Bob was not interested in being called, "First Gentleman or First Man," or any other titles. He would not take on the roles of party planner and menu selector as the former presidents' wives had done for events held in the president's house. People started calling him "Dr. Bob," which he liked and adopted.

My husband, Bob Canady, and I ride together in the homecoming parade.

Because Bob is a former professor, he knew a great deal about universities, but he was not interested in a faculty appointment. A former college athlete, he knew about coaches and athletic departments, but he did not want to be thought of as an athletic fundraiser, a suggestion made to him. His first and foremost role was my husband and supporter, but he was willing to participate in university events, engage with the community, and convey positive messages about what he learned.

One of his major functions was to play in golf tournaments that supported various sports and many non-profit organizations. It was customary for the president to play in these tournaments. In my first visits to the city, I was asked, "Will you play in our golf tournaments?" I said, "No, but Bob will." Bob was not a golfer when this question was asked of me in late January, so he had until July when we moved to Memphis to become one. A terrific athlete, I was sure he could play golf, so we quickly arranged lessons while still living in Lexington. Bob grew to love the game, almost as much as he enjoyed telling the golf teams how I got him started in golf. They commented that they knew he was new to the game, but he was a hit because of his enjoyment and jovial, not too serious, approaches to tournament play.

Dr. Bob gained prominence in 12 churches around the Memphis area. In his retirement, Bob returned to his first love, art, and became a stained glass artist. He had designed, created and installed stained glass windows for Trinity Hills Methodist Church in Lexington and another Methodist church in Frankfort, Kentucky.

When we moved to Memphis and Bob's talents became known, he was asked to create stained glass windows for several churches. He had one caveat. The churches to which he donated the stained glass windows must not be able to afford them. The stained glass windows became his gift to the churches, many of which were in African-American communities. Mark Stansbury, an executive assistant from my office, worked with Bob and arranged introductions to churches that met Bob's criteria.

From the initial announcement of my appointment, the introductions to legendary leaders, the receptions and early reactions, it was clear that as president of the University of Memphis, I would be a prominent figure in the Memphis community. The early interactions were exhilarating. Bob's engagement with the university and the community was met with acceptance and appreciation. Our beginning "Walking in Memphis" time cemented my belief that the University and the City of Memphis were inextricably tied and that both needed each other to prosper. The next phase was to finalize the leadership team and start to walk the walk in Memphis.

A proud day in their lives. Father and Mother dressed for a lunch with the governor before my inauguration ceremony.

BUILDING LEADERSHIP

When I became president of the University of Memphis, my immediate concern was to decide which members of the leadership team I inherited should remain and which ones to replace. The President's Council, my direct reports, had functional responsibility for the planning, organization, management, and leadership of various divisions of the university.

Beneath them on the organizational chart were numerous other leaders with responsibility for this vast educational endeavor that employed about 2,500 faculty and staff and enrolled between 22,000 and 23,000 students who aspired to earn bachelor's, master's, and doctoral degrees. Six major divisions, numerous departments, centers, institutes, and foundations were managed by people with titles and leadership responsibilities.

Regardless of gender or race, from my previous experiences with effective leaders, the most important attributes of a successful leader are trust, integrity, and abilities to communicate, cooperate, and collaborate well. The prerequisite knowledge, skills, and experiences were givens.

By the time I had interviewed the vice presidents and directors, I knew how they were perceived by the people they supervised. I had already learned that they were thought to be trustworthy and that they were considered people of integrity. They were trusted at least by the people in their divisions. For the university's well-being and my success as president, all on my leadership team also had to be trusted and respected across the other divisions, across campus, and in the community.

> *Senior leadership team members must have the knowledge, expertise, and experience relevant to their position. But just as important, they must have integrity and consistently practice good communication, cooperation, and collaboration, thereby engendering trust on their teams and other parts of the organization.*

Eventually, I wanted all employees with supervisory titles to consider themselves as leaders and to embrace the vision, plans, and changes in culture the President's Council and I wanted to adopt. However, my first challenge was to determine if I had the right administrators on the President's Council, the right leaders on the leadership team.

COMMUNICATION

Often when I interviewed people who aspired to become leaders on campus, I asked about their backgrounds in previous jobs. However, I also was interested in what steps on their career paths and characteristics helped them achieve their present level of leadership. Invariably, the ability to communicate effectively was a trait I found among the best leaders.

When administrators communicate effectively with each other, there is a spirit of goodwill. When teams of labor and management embrace whatever the challenge is, people enjoy their work, and the organization as a whole functions well.

Coming to terms with poor communication. After a few weekly President's Council meetings, it became clear that communication problems existed between two of my senior leaders. I observed that communications in group settings lacked open and honest sharing of their division's issues and challenges, a prerequisite when group input is needed to make decisions.

I had individual meetings with each supervisor about the issue. I had face-to-face meetings with both of them at once. I held team-building retreats. Nothing produced consistent improvement between the men and the poor communication and distrust had rubbed off on the employees of both their divisions.

Finally, I called them both into my office and said, "I am leaving you here in my office for you to come to an understanding about specifics of how you will communicate with each other and how you will encourage communication and collaboration on projects between your divisions." I left my office, went across campus to a meeting, and returned in about an hour. When I heard a productive discussion going on, I exited again and told them I would be back in another hour to hear their collective plan.

Suffice it to say, conditions improved, or one or both of them would have been relieved of their duties. I did not threaten them with job loss, but I did say that my evaluation of each of them was low at this time because of the poor communications I had observed. I directed them to select a university problem that needed to be addressed across their two divisions and that required members of their teams to work together. Eventually, they worked it out.

Opening a new avenue of communication creates loyalty, support, and collaboration. Setting up for recruitment fairs on campus required arranging and rearranging tables, chairs, bandstands with sound and lights, IT equipment, decorations, food service, hotel accommodations, parking, and communication materials representing all of the majors, the student organizations, etc. These events were not the favorite activities of the physical plant employees because it added significantly to their regular duties. Yet, when we had a big event on campus, such as a recruitment fair, it was all hands on deck, whether it was their usual jobs or not.

One year we decided to increase the number of recruitment fairs from one to three. We wanted to attract more people to make a campus visit because we knew that if potential students visited our campus, they were more likely to enroll. We needed to grow enrollment because we had been accomplishing our goals of graduating more students every year. We had to replace those graduates with new students.

We decided to have three recruitment fairs to showcase our beautiful campus. The campus visit required faculty and staff at tables to talk about majors to prospective students. The visitors also enjoyed interacting with leaders in student government. A variety of student organizations were represented, and campus guides assisted the potential students. We also set up an outside stage for performances by "Sound Fusion," our student rock band.

I heard from some of my inner office staff that the physical plant people were not happy about the expansion from one on-campus recruitment fair to three. My office assistant even warned me that the physical plant employees, who had previously been supportive of me, were now exhibiting mounting resentment at the extra work.

We called a hasty meeting and gathered the physical plant employees in the Rose Theatre. I communicated our rationale for having three recruitment fairs. I emphasized how significant their work was, stating that they and many others on campus were keys to our success of enrolling more students, not just the recruiters or the faculty members, but all of us. The landscapers who made the campus beautiful, the housing employees who prepared the residence halls for the new visitors, the plumbers who kept the fountains and facilities going, the decorators and caterers—all were necessary for us to create a good impression. It was a massive organizational project, one we would need to repeat two more times.

I heard a man say as he left the meeting, "I'm an engineer. I did not sign up for the job to move tables." Immediately, I approached him, but before I could say anything, a woman replied, "Well, I know we need to grow enrollment. I want to keep my job and even hire more people for my team. She can count on me. More students mean more job security." I could have hugged her; she communicated my message exactly.

We had a great recruitment fair, the first of three. Sound Fusion rocked, the food was delicious, and parents, grandparents, school counselors, and students came from many different parts of the country. As promised, I was there to help set up the equipment, and as exhausted as I was from talking non-stop to so many people, making speeches, and serving as host for the events, I was determined to be there for the breakdown of the equipment as I had been for the setup.

After that first event was over, I walked into the Rose Theatre and saw

Establish communications that include all the stakeholders in your organization. This will help all necessary personnel understand the rationale for a decision, buy into the actions, and share in the success.

a row of physical plant people resting. I sat down beside a man I had seen around campus. I recognized him by the red cap he always wore.

"Dr. Raines, did we get our numbers?" he asked.

"Do you mean the number of students we need?"

He nodded.

"We won't know until the enrollment period is over, but I promise to keep you informed."

And, I did. I communicated directly with Mr. Red Cap and all of the physical plant employees. After each of the recruitment fairs, I sent the whole campus a message about how much I appreciated the extra effort the physical plant employees made in setting up the grounds for our recruitment fairs and reminded everyone that these events helped boost enrollment.

Sometime later I sought their advice about how to make the fairs even better. They suggested how to make the logistics, parking, and flow of the crowd more efficient. They were invested in improvement of the event because they too had a stake in whether we "got our numbers." Routinely, I expanded my communications on campus-wide concerns to include the physical plant employees, which had not happened before the recruitment fairs challenge.

When we as leaders ask people to help us meet a challenge, they buy in, become engaged in the process, and appreciate knowing the good reasons they are being asked to do more.

With the President's Council and with my support staff in the president's office, I had some difficult, gut-wrenching decisions to make, usually about people or budgets. However, I seldom made the decisions in isolation without information and feedback from others. I needed the cooperation of my team and their collaboration to provide the data, break down the barriers, and work across divisions for common purposes.

We needed excellent communication and collaboration across the enterprise. We needed the Business and Finance division to collaborate with Academic Affairs. We needed Academic Affairs to collaborate with IT and Business and Finance to handle the new enterprise system we installed. We needed to collaborate on finding ways for our students to graduate technologically savvy in their fields of study. And on and on.

TRUST

Trust is derived when we perceive each other as trustworthy. Leaders on my team had to perform their duties well and interact well with people in their divisions, with each other, and with me. In the beginning months of working together, the team members already knew each other, but they needed to get to know me quickly because the business of the university was immediate. We were obligated to serve our students well, and the employees in each division were counting on us.

Trust is deeply rooted. We build our reputations by doing more than is required and by not letting people down. But trust is fragile and can be lost.

One person I trusted to lead an important project seemed to be just the right person. He had the qualifications, got along well with others, and seemed to relish being

Demand trustworthiness in your organization. Make sure employees know that they are being trusted to do what is right, get the job done, and communicate results to everyone who needs to know. And hold them accountable.

selected to lead the project. Although he began the project immediately in an almost boastful manner, he soon tired of the daily responsibilities. He ignored the details of the project and let the schedule slip. In addition, he did not tell me the truth about the status of the project. I recalled a statement my mother used to say: "Can do and will do are two different things."

After a heated confrontation in my office, I told the project leader directly that I had lost faith and trust in him and would assign the project to someone else.

Can Trust Be Regained? Should People Get a Second Chance?

The man looked at me directly and asked, "What can I do to regain your trust?" His question took me off-guard. I said I was not sure and asked him to return the next day to discuss it. I needed time to think it through.

> *Ensure the establishment of rules, guidelines, procedures, modus operandi, and standard operating procedures. Hold people accountable. But, also do not lose the ability to temper your judgment by giving second chances.*

I decided to give him another chance. I directed him to finish the project on time and within budget and to ensure each detail of the work was completed accurately. And, to make sure he stayed on track, I required him to report his progress to me weekly.

After that, I have seldom seen a person work as hard and effectively as he did. However, I kept a closer eye on his work to make sure my decision was wise. (See references for Cummings' book on second chances.)

Word soon spread that the project was back on track and that I had given the leader a second chance. At first, I was concerned that people who were just coming to know me might interpret my decision as something a weak, easily deceived female might do and that they would expect do-overs for every failed action. I vowed to keep closer tabs on major projects and intervene as soon as a project showed signs of running into trouble.

Relieving people of their leadership titles or prominent roles in projects, or firing them outright, are not actions any good leader enjoys. Giving this person a second chance but holding him strictly accountable demonstrated that I was fair but firm. This course of action was a benefit to the man and to the university. I am glad I gave him a second chance because in any organization, with every team, there will always be those who deserve a second chance and can be motivated to become outstanding leaders.

Trusted with Financial Responsibilities. One of the duties I agreed to when I was sworn in as president was fiduciary. That meant that I was to conduct myself in a way that would safeguard the funds and holdings of the university. As an individual employee, I was responsible for the fiduciary performance of the university as a whole. That was a sobering and solemn responsibility that I always took very seriously.

I had to assess whether the people I placed in trust of the university's assets had the necessary knowledge, training, and skills to handle their financial responsibilities. And, assess whether they were trustworthy.

We set in place financial controls to help safeguard assets. Nevertheless, I sometimes learned that someone had mishandled finances. We recognized the financial wrongs through reports from auditors, personnel in business and finance departments, the suspected employee's supervisors, HR, legal counsel, or the police. In universities as in corporations, people sometimes defraud the organization, even embezzle funds. People who managed grants were relieved of their directorships when they misused funds. At other times, people unintentionally made mistakes through a lack of training or understanding. Whatever the situation, a rapid and decisive response was required. That was part of my fiduciary duty.

As administrators and leaders, when something goes wrong or someone does wrong, we often question our judgment. We ask ourselves why we didn't see it coming. We have a tendency to blame ourselves when we are not really at fault. (See Myers' book about dealing with financial crisis.)

Overall, we were successful in meeting our financial responsibilities during my presidency. One of the awards of which I am most proud was given to our administration by the Tennessee Higher Education Commission and reported in a proclamation from the General Assembly when I retired. My administration and I were recognized as respected throughout the state for our management and fiscal responsibility.

INSPIRATION

Most leaders in higher education feel a deep commitment to the academic life, to their students, to the traditions of various disciplines, to the knowledge we are asked to transmit, and the learning experiences we provide. We are entrusted by society with transmitting the societal and cultural values, and knowledge that is inherent in the education process. We have many lofty goals, but the work is difficult and the demands great, so we must stay inspired.

Inspired leadership is a lofty goal, but it is often practiced through performance of less than lofty tasks. I recall the case of Adam, an intern who worked with us for four years. When he graduated, we gave him a party, and he gave the office a gift. He explained that the framed quote reflected what he would always remember about working in the president's office. The quote read, "Happiness is doing with a smile what you have to do anyway." It was an anonymous quote from a daily office calendar.

As Adam handed me the gift, he smiled and said, . . . "without bitching and moaning." He said he didn't think it would be appropriate to add those words to the framed quote, but we got his meaning. In every office, in every division, throughout the university, there are those tasks that must be done. It would be best to do them as Adam suggested.

Where does inspiration come from? Inspiration may come from devotion to our mission, to our students. Or, it may arise on a more personal level from our religious beliefs, our need for creative expression, or our drive to make a better life for our children or grandchildren. I knew employees who stayed on the job because their teams got to build Habitat for Humanity houses. Some teams lived for the "Up Til Dawn" event to raise funds for the St. Jude Research Hospital in Memphis. Other teams worked every year to assist with the Salvation Army Angel Tree gifts at Christmas.

We must seek some inspiration from our actual work, whatever it is. Being asked to lead a project that challenges our organizational skills may be inspiring. Long-held friendships with co-workers may be a source of inspiration. On a more personal level, we may be inspired because the company or the university gives us the opportunity to learn more, and we are hungry to learn.

For many people making a difference is their inspiration.

If we are inspired to get up in the morning, go to our workplaces, function as part of a team, and help solve problems, then we are difference makers in our organizations. We all deserve to know that we are needed and that we are making our working lives and others' lives better.

In conclusion

Trust, trustworthiness, integrity, veracity, and reliability are attributes of an effective leader of an organization. Trust is earned, sometimes quickly. At other times, more experiences of working together longer are need to develop trust.

We who desire to become better leaders seek new knowledge. It is the seekers, the inspired ones, the responsible ones, who take their organizations and themselves into a better future together with their employees. We make the conscious efforts to communicate, cooperate, and collaborate.

Chapter 9

CREATING THE STRUCTURE
FOR SUCCESS

NAMES AND SYMBOLS MATTER

Universities, like all institutions, change with the times, but we draw strength from our roots. Founded in 1912, the University of Memphis had always been a public university. Five times the university's name changed, and its mission expanded. First, it was called West Tennessee Normal School from 1912 to 1925; West Tennessee State Teachers College from 1925 to 1941; Memphis State College from 1941 to 1957; Memphis State University from 1957 to 1994; and the University of Memphis from 1994 to today.

The change from Memphis State College to Memphis State University in 1957 was especially significant because it recognized that our institution had become a graduate degree-granting university while remaining strong in undergraduate education. Then, in the

1970s, we were classified as a doctoral extensive research university. Names and classifications matter to faculty, donors, and funding agencies. My challenge to the research faculty was to generate $100 million in research dollars each year, a threshold that many funding agencies use as an indicator that we are able to handle large research studies. However, the $100 million mark is difficult to achieve without a medical school as a part of the university.

Early on in my presidency, when I spoke with individual alums, many still referred to the university as Memphis State. At first I corrected them, but then I learned to let it go because I heard the misnomer so often. However, when some famous announcers on national television called us Memphis State while broadcasting our basketball games in the NCAA tournament, we did not let that gaffe go. Immediately, our sports information officer was on the phone to the network.

One name I never let anyone call us without a vigorous defense was "Tiger High." On one occasion, I was in an outpatient clinic to undergo a routine test for which I would be sedated. The anesthesiologist's assistant who was to give me the sedative said, "I hear you are the president of the university." Then he said, "I'm a graduate of Tiger High."

I said, "Pardon me, where is that?" I knew what he was referring to because I had heard that name before. He said, "Oh, that's just what we call the university because it is like going to a high school for those of us who drove into campus, not like going away to a real college." Outraged, I asked him when was the last time he had been on campus? How many students live on campus? What is our enrollment? What is our graduation rate? What public campus in the State of Tennessee is rated as the safest by TBI, the Tennessee Bureau of Investigation? Who has the highest passing rate on the bar? What are the rankings for the nursing program, speech-language pathology program, education programs, and engineering college? Who has the largest honors program in the state?

Of course, he could not answer any of the questions, except what the win/loss record was for our basketball team. I was in the process of answering all of the questions for him. He was late giving me the sedative because I would not stop talking. Finally, he said, "You are making me late for my next patient. Usually, patients talk while they are under sedation, but you're still talking, and I haven't given it to you yet." I replied, "I will make a deal with you if you promise never to call the University of Memphis 'Tiger High,' I will take the sedative and get you back on schedule."

Protection of the University of Memphis's very name and our image and reputation became one of my major responsibilities to students, faculty, staff, citizens of Memphis, our state, and our nation.

Protecting one's good name as a leader is the basis for your individual image and reputation and that in turn has a profound effect on the organization's image and reputation. As the senior executive officer, you are the face of the organization.

A PROBING QUESTION

In a board meeting of the Board of Visitors (BOV), interim chair John Kelley bluntly asked me, "What is your vision for the University of Memphis?" I squirmed and said, "I am not sure yet." The room grew very quiet, and than I broke the silence by saying, "But I will have an announcement soon. We are finishing our work on a formal statement." While that was true, the vision for my leadership team and me was not yet crystal clear. There were so many things we wanted to accomplish to make the university better. However, I needed to move beyond ambiguity and give a precisely worded proclamation of our vision and our agenda of exciting changes.

The President's Council and I were armed with the data and impressions from all our meetings with deans and faculty members from the schools, colleges, libraries, centers, and institutes. I was aware of the perceptions of the university from various segments of the community. I had gleaned a variety of perceptions from my visits to churches, speeches at civic organizations and alumni groups, interviews of directors of foundations, and meetings with individual Board of Visitors members. In addition, I had regular meetings with the presidents and vice presidents of the faculty and staff senates, as well as the officers of the Student Government Association. We dealt with a dizzying volume of data and perceptions. We shared academic values, and those became the foundation for our vision, mission, and goal statements.

First, we were deeply committed to our mission as a public research university to provide our community and region with high-quality education, research results, and public service. In a number of retreats, on and off campus, and in meeting after meeting as the President's Council, we hammered out our vision, mission, and strategic goals. We were determined that the strategic plan would not be a document on the shelf, but rather a living document that accurately reflected who we were, where we were, and where we were going.

VISION STATEMENT

"The University of Memphis will be recognized as one of America's great metropolitan research universities, noted for its comprehensive, innovative academic programs and for capitalizing on its urban setting and the region to address the challenges of our global society."

In all of our deliberations, we had intentionally emphasized that we would be recognized as one of America's great metropolitan research universities. Our university suffered somewhat from the long shadow cast from the eastern side of the state by the University of Tennessee, a land grant university. There were those who also thought it was limiting to have a name associated with a city, rather than with the whole state. We needed our identity to be the metropolitan research university that would capitalize on our metropolitan and urban settings.

We have a beautiful campus, not downtown, and we had more resources than many of the struggling universities with cities attached to their names. Fortunately, we also had some high-quality peers, such as the University of Pittsburgh, University of Cincinnati, University of Louisville, and University of Alabama at Birmingham, to name some we sought to gauge ourselves against. A definite limiting factor was that we did not have a medical school, which many city-associated universities did. A medical school was located in Memphis, but it was the University of Tennessee's medical school. Medical schools generate a significant amount of research funding, making comparisons with some of the other universities more difficult. Our job was to define our strengths and build on them.

MISSION STATEMENT

Our adopted mission statement was the following: "The University of Memphis is a learner-centered metropolitan research university providing high-quality education experiences while pursuing new knowledge through research, artistic expression, and interdisciplinary and engaged scholarship." At the time, the emphasis on interdisciplinary and engaged scholarship was a term few people used in academic circles.

Major Goals

We adopted six major goals.

1. Student Success: Provide distinctive learning experiences that foster lifelong success.

2. Research and Creativity: Cultivate the scholarship of discovery, integration, application, and teaching to advance knowledge and enhance society.

3. Access and Diversity: Promote and sustain an accessible, vibrant community that values diversity.

4. Partnerships: Cultivate relationships which link the mission of the University to external communities.

5. Campus Culture and Service Excellence: Create a campus culture that advances shared governance and sustains and supports operational and service excellence.

6. Sense of Place: Develop an inviting and sustainable campus setting.

While we had multiple unveilings of the vision, mission, and major goals, with discussions among faculty, staff, and students, it was the unveiling with the BOV members that was most revealing. The BOV business leaders were accustomed to writing and living strategic plans in their businesses.

Mr. Kelley, the interim BOV chair, and the BOV members were excited about a vision of the University of Memphis as one of America's great metropolitan research universities. The phrases "service excellence" and "linking the university to external communities" resonated with them partly because they were the products of sessions with our staff. They appreciated our plans when we announced that each division and all colleges and units of the university would devise their own plans to be congruent with the university's overall mission, vision, and goals. We would devise metrics to define each unit's success. These distinguished business and political leaders on the BOV grew to understand the vastness of expectations and ways of operating our complex organization.

In the following years, our President's Council developed five themes that guided all of our work and that resonated throughout the university:

1. Investing in people
2. Building productive partnerships
3. Creating interdisciplinary initiatives
4. Enhancing our image and reputation
5. Developing new resources

This last theme was added during a retreat when we learned that funding for higher education would receive no increases in the state's budget. In fact, our budget was cut because of low state revenues, almost a prediction of what would happen in 2008 when the recession started.

The five themes became the bedrock of our work as a leadership team. They appeared in my speeches and were expressions of the culture we were striving to develop. Some concrete examples of each of the themes follow.

Investing in People. When I arrived on campus, a quick analysis showed we had too many temporary or interim titles. Faculty members were leaving the university at a rate much higher than the national turnover rate. With the division heads and vice presidents, we reviewed the job performance of the temporary and interim appointments. We assessed whether or not we had the appropriate leaders in the positions.

Secondly, we looked at every faculty position that had been vacated and determined why. We wanted to know where the faculty member was going and why he or she had chosen to leave. We received some information from formal inquiry and other insights from informal discussions. We learned about the problems in the units, including some of the leaders. For example, in our review of the philosophy department, we found that the Ivy League universities had been raiding our faculty because of our excellent reputation and because we had more minority faculty members than most philosophy departments. We found that some people in the College of Business and Economics left because of their insecurity with a revolving door of deans. This problem was rectified when we appointed John Pepin for a five-year term. In the College of Education, we found some faculty members leaving for lower-ranked universities because they felt insecure about the promotion and tenure process at a research university such as ours.

Whatever the reasons, we needed to "invest in people," the right faculty and administrators, as well as invest in training the appointed leaders in how to be supportive of the people who reported to them. We consciously tried to keep the best, the most promising people who had the potential to become campus leaders. These comments should not imply that we had wholesale departures. We did not. But the trend needed to be reversed. When it became apparent that the President's Council and I took seriously the "investing in people" theme, which soon we began calling the "people and leader" issues, we found that our faculty and staff stayed even when recruiters from other places called. The ones who stayed became our advocates.

For example, Dr. Art Graesser, a well-known psychologist and artificial intelligence expert, was recruited by a number of other universities. He decided to stay despite attempts by other universities to recruit him. News soon spread of Art's decision to stay. We were then able to retain other valuable experts, grant generators, and people we valued for their leadership skills.

Faculty members were not the only ones we needed to convince to stay. Some professional staff members also were highly recruited. A key to our future success was improved technology on campus, particularly for research purposes. Technology staff members were often recruited by industry at salaries we could not match, but our culture of respect, opportunities to grow, and our announced intentions to improve our enterprise system often convinced them to stay.

Our investments in faculty and staff members paid dividends beyond our imaginations. Our loyalty to the people who taught the students, conducted research, and served the community well was repaid by accomplishments reaching far beyond what we had envisioned.

Building Productive Partnerships. Eventually, the theme of "building productive partnerships" expanded to include "on and off" the campus. "Building productive partnerships" was a phrase used often in my introductions for speeches to civic groups. We added the theme of "community connectedness" as we sought to engage our faculty in research projects that mattered to the community. Also, we wanted to engage our students in meaningful projects and sustain efforts that made the university a true partner with the community, not just a flash in the pan partner for a study. Daily, I sought to engage our university with the city and the region.

Providing service and leadership on boards proved to be one avenue for influence that led to productive, sustainable partnerships between the university and community. For example, with the help of Stephanie Beasley from my office, I served on the:

- Board of the Methodist-Le Bonheur Healthcare System that resulted in a partnership with our Loewenberg School of Nursing.

- Memphis Chamber of Commerce Board (Chair), which led to a partnership with our Fogelman College of Business and Economics;

- Public Television Board, which partnered with our School of Communications and Fine Arts;

- Memphis Tomorrow Board, that championed early childhood education and that led to a partnership with the College of Education and to an initiative on criminal justice with our School of Urban Affairs and Public Policy.

- Memphis Gateway Committee for the Aerotropolis initiative (Chair), which encompassed the airport and surrounding community, led to a partnership with our program in Architecture and the university's landscape designers.

The university's Research Foundation Board also leveraged proposals from university faculty entrepreneurs into start-up businesses in the community, such as a water testing company and some medical devices. In speeches and writing, I told the stories of the success of University of Memphis faculty members and students in devising ways to help our community. The responsibility to educate students and leaders for the good of society was a deeply held value. It meant, however, that I needed to know our faculty and their expertise extremely well.

At every annual awards banquet for each college and school, accreditation visits, or public lectures, I was not the president who escaped as soon as possible after being introduced. I had seen that model, and it was offensive to me when I was a faculty member. At special meetings and events, I was determined to interact with people, learn about programs, and seek to be involved with issues.

Consider the awards celebrations as opportunities to build connections between senior leaders and employees at all levels.

Creating Interdisciplinary Initiatives. Perhaps the most inventive of our interdisciplinary initiatives arose from frustration. I was annoyed that my counterparts at the University of Tennessee Health Sciences Center were not willing to work with us in the area of public health, a major concern in the Delta, the Mid-South, and Memphis. We often came to the brink of a partnership between the two institutions that would have been a historic agreement for the state. However, the UT officials pulled out of a final agreement several times when changes in their administration occurred.

Exasperated by the lack of cooperation in building a partnership, we investigated beginning our own U of M School of Public Health. With the assistance of Dr. David Cox, we reviewed the guidelines for accreditation from the Council of Education for Public Health (CEPH). Throughout the university, we had most of the faculty with the expertise to deliver the required components of the CEPH standards.

With the approval of the Tennessee Board of Regents and the Tennessee Higher Education Commission, we established the University of Memphis's School of Public Health by bringing together faculty members with expertise from different departments throughout the university to work on our most ambitious "interdisciplinary initiative." We assembled faculty members in health care economics, administration, and public health nursing. A National Institute of

Health grantee, Dr. Lisa Klegses, became our first dean.

Recruiting the right people and creating a workable structure for the School of Public Health and for CEPH accreditation were as crucial as the need for resources. The Ayers Foundation, headed by Jim and Janet Ayers, were acutely aware that public health was a critical issue for our region. The Assisi Foundation, led by Jan Young, and the Plough Foundation, chaired by Diane Rudner, provided additional funding.

We formed an excellent advisory board and obtained additional funding from Blue Cross Blue Shield of Tennessee and from Cigna Health Insurance. The hospitals in the area, particularly Methodist Le Bonheur, its former president, Maurice Elliott, CEO Gary Shorb, and Steve Reynolds of Baptist Healthcare were instrumental in making sure we were facing the critical public health issues of our region. But, it was Yvonne Madlock, the 20-year veteran director of the Shelby County Health Department, who was the reality test for all of our endeavors. Shelby County was at the heart of public health needs. With the nation grappling with healthcare issues such as smoking-induced diseases, childhood obesity, opioid and other drug addictions, we did not have time to waste.

Our School of Public Health was successful at building interdisciplinary programs and recruiting students for our master's and doctoral degree programs. I often felt I was pouring my drive, intellect, and energy into something we could not allow to fail because our community, the Delta region, and the Mid-South needed the knowledgeable people we could provide. The continuation of the School of Public Health remains one of the accomplishments I value most during my tenure.

Be bold and take the lead. Design the programs the community needs and don't look back at the hindrances, look forward to the opportunities.

Enhancing Our Image and Reputation. Symbols and icons matter as promoters of image and reputation. When I became president, the widely used crest of our university included a paddle wheeler. That image connoted times gone by rather than the intellectual pursuits that were our real marks of distinction.

Our office of Communications and Marketing shield project, led by Linda Bonnin, unveiled an extraordinary new academic crest rendered in blue on silver, which approximated our school colors of blue and gray. The Latin inscription, "Imaginari, Cognitari, and Facere," corresponded closely with our university motto of "Dreamers, Thinkers, Doers."

The new crest was received with great enthusiasm. We used it on marquees, banners, badges for the band, campus police officers' uniforms, business cards, letterheads, and eventually on vehicles and signs leading into the campus. It seemed that everyone wanted a lapel pin with the new crest.

The academic crest that helped modernize the image of the university.

At speaking engagements, I gave out pins. They were worn proudly by members of the Board of Visitors and the National Alumni Association Board, civic organization officers, and most importantly, employees. I handed out pins to university employees at ceremonies for their work anniversaries and especially at celebrations for "service excellence." Each member of my leadership team and the president's office staff were asked to wear the pins at all times. If someone in an audience deserved or just asked for a pin, I often gave mine away or "stole" one from the lapel of one of the vice presidents. The vice presidents and other members of the leadership team soon adopted the practice and gave pins to their audiences, as well.

When we appointed Bob Eoff as vice president, we charged him with enhancing our image and reputation. One of Bob's great assets was his television background. He had a sense of news urgency and timing that few university personnel possessed. Bob and his small video crew collected numerous great stories illustrating our motto.

Bob helped me craft my message and launched videos and TV commercials that reflected positive goodwill. In promotional spots on television, in print for distribution to prospective students, in everyday correspondence, and in the conclusions of presentations, my proud declaration was, "We are Dreamers, Thinkers, Doers." We knew we were gaining success when we began hearing others use our motto all over town.

Developing New Resources. Great universities have great alumni associations, well-developed foundations, and leaders who can reach deep into the community and tap the goodwill of alumni living there. The result can be new resources.

Reportedly, several previous administrators believed that because U of M is a public university, state funding would provide for our needs. From my experience at universities in other states and in Tennessee, I knew that this belief was mistaken. Reports in *The Chronicle of Higher Education* and from the Association of Public and Land-grant Universities (APLU) indicated that public universities had declined to the point of becoming not publicly funded universities but rather "state-assisted universities." We analyzed our own data and determined we were in the latter category. State universities have often been lambasted in public meetings and in the news media for increasing tuition. That's because few people recognize that tuition increases are necessitated by decreasing state support.

I found it abominable to hear legislators and sometimes the news media criticize us for increasing tuition when it was the state that cut our budgets. Our most realistic alternative was to win additional support from our alumni, many of whom heard from us only at the annual fundraising time. We needed more contacts and more support from alumni, foundations, and grants and contracts.

Spreading the word. The theme of "developing additional resources" became linked to "enhancing image and reputation." Many of our alumni did not know the deans and departments chairs in the college from which they graduated. I met alumni when I attended meetings or gave speeches at multiple civic organization meetings and at Tiger Club meetings of fans of our various sports teams. Whether alumni or not, Memphis residents would always turn out when a head basketball coach, football coach, or athletic director was scheduled to speak. I ambushed the usual athletic presentation with brief remarks about some academic area of the university. I reported a few facts about some great recognition the university had received. At public lectures held by the College of Business and Economics, I would sprinkle my introductory remarks with news such as the following: The Cecil C. Humphreys School of Law has the highest passing rate on the bar of any law school in the state; the Speech and Hearing Program is ranked in the top ten in the nation; or the College of Education is recognized nationally for its preparation of teachers to serve special-needs students.

Becoming more effective at telling our success stories was a key to attracting the attention and resources from alumni, donors, and foundations. In industry, an increase in the marketing and communications budget would have been considered appropriate; however, the shortsighted guidelines of the Tennessee Board of Regents stipulated that university resources could not be used for marketing.

Alumni resources. We decided to ask the alumni association to provide funding to promote the university and its accomplishments. But first, we had to revamp the alumni association.

Early on in my administration, we proposed a plan that included forming a national association with its own board to replace the loosely knitted confederation of local clubs. Under the leadership of Richard Glassman and Dawn Graeter, we appointed a university-funded position for a director of the alumni association. This change was a turning point in our success. We selected Tammy Hedges, an energetic and enthusiastic person, who had the ability to plan and execute engaging public events that were the talk of the town. The annual alumni awards banquets had unusual themes and were held in unexpected places like airplane hangars, the lobby of a guitar factory, and the zoo. The annual alumni events were the most creative events I have experienced anywhere. The creativity and ingenuity made the events memorable, but the staff's interactions with the alumni and with the leadership of the national board cemented our enhanced image and reputation.

Foundation resources. The restructuring of the alumni association had enhanced our image and reputation, but we needed another restructuring. The University of Memphis Foundation's operations were ones that should have been undertaken separately from my activities at the university. However, the inadequate functioning, the few professional personnel trained in fundraising, and the lack of resources meant that the university had to work on this restructuring and present it to the board.

Whatever the organizational structure, determine the resource streams. Every leader needs people and financial resources, and they can be organized in a variety of ways.

We needed the University of Memphis Foundation to succeed in soliciting, accepting, managing, and investing resources. We appointed Julie Johnson as foundation director. She had the requisite background in fundraising, the winning personality, and the desire to succeed.

GOVERNANCE ISSUES CONTINUED

Our strategic plan was working. Our themes and goals were reflected in our accomplishments. Our motto was in the minds of citizens, alumni, and donors. We had created a Research Foundation, reshaped the Alumni Association into a national organization with a board, and restructured the University of Memphis Foundation with appropriate bylaws, fiduciary responsibilities, and experienced administrators and fund-raisers. Throughout these efforts, the goodwill and support of the Board of Visitors made it possible for us to accomplish these tasks. I considered our Board of Visitors like a Board of Trustees, even though the legal authority for governance of the University of Memphis rested in Nashville with the Tennessee Board of Regents.

The University of Memphis and I benefited from the guidance of Dr. Charles Manning, Chancellor of the Tennessee Board of Regents and later from Chancellor John Morgan. Meetings with other presidents were helpful when we shared ideas and reviewed state policies and regulations. TBR's professional staff in academic affairs, buildings and facilities, business and finance, government relations, information systems, and legal counsel provided added expertise to that of our campus administrators.

Long before I became president, the Board of Visitors had lobbied governors and legislators for the University of Memphis to have its own governing board like the University of Tennessee. They felt that a group appointed in Nashville with only one or two people from Memphis did not adequately represent the vast needs and interests of Memphis. At the time, Memphis was the largest city in the state. They also thought that if the University of Memphis had its own Board of Trustees, people would be more likely to make donations.

I served under three governors—Don Sundquist, Phil Bredesen, and Bill Haslam—and the case was made for a Memphis governing board without success until Governor Haslam made the decision. His family members were major philanthropists in Knoxville and major donors to the University of Tennessee. He understood the significance of the community and donations to universities.

On December 1, 2015, Governor Bill Haslam announced plans to create a separate Board of Trustees for the University of Memphis. While his announcement came two years after I had left the university, Interim President Brad Martin and M. David Rudd, the new president, continued the drive. However, rather than simply designate a new board for the University of Memphis for which we had petitioned, Governor Haslam announced that all six of the universities in the Tennessee Board of Regents would be allowed to have their own boards, an unanticipated consequence of the independent board request.

Tennessee Governor Bill Haslam discussing higher education issues with me.

Chapter 10

RESOURCEFULNESS AND PERSEVERANCE FOR LEGENDARY PROJECTS

Buildings and campus designs can endure long beyond the lifetimes of those who create them. They become symbols of what a university campus represents to the students, faculty, staff, and community. Functional design of structures and spaces can enhance learning.

Organizing functional offices to serve students better is a statement of values. Redesigning the campus plan to purposefully group students together, academically and socially, is a tactic to strengthen opportunities for learning. Providing access to the campus for the community is a symbol of a welcoming environment and a means for strengthening community connections.

Funds spent on buildings always sparked controversy because many employees felt salaries and benefits should be improved first. I often agreed with them; however, funds for personnel and benefits came from different state accounts and had explicit state policy constraints. Our campus had many outdated buildings requiring major maintenance and renovations, and some needed to be replaced altogether. We accommodated renovation changes through the university's recurring budget, but new buildings required matching funds.

Governor Phil Bredesen, as Chair of the Tennessee Board of Regents (TBR), required universities to raise matching funds to access state funds. The College of Business and Economics and the Athletics Department had many more donors and were able to raise matching funds more readily. The other colleges, libraries, institutes, and centers wondered if they would ever have their needs met through the matching funds approach.

In the annual fundraising campaigns, we purposefully drew attention to academic space and facility needs, as well as athletics. Later as a part of the "100th Anniversary Empowering the Dream Campaign," we identified donors interested in the various academic programs and buildings.

CAMPUS MASTER PLAN AND REDESIGNS

Every university campus in the state had a master plan. When I arrived in 2001, we were working from a 1998 plan. Five years later in 2006, and then again in 2013, we developed the extensive campus master redesigns. Annually, we were required to relate the plans to the campus master plan. As these public documents were filed, we were in direct competition for higher education funding with the other TBR universities, community colleges and technical schools, as well as the campuses of the University of Tennessee system. TBR and the Tennessee Higher Education Commission (THEC) resolved issues of priorities among the construction projects for all of the state's higher education institutions.

With strong leadership from the department of Campus Planning and Design, the Physical Plant, and Business and Finance, our plans always were approved. We accomplished an aggressive campus update, despite a budget freeze in 2001 and several years of low state appropriations because of low state tax revenues. The most significant recession of 2008 forced us to rethink a number of initiatives, including funding for buildings. Thankfully, 2003 and 2010 were significant dates for completions of major building projects begun years earlier.

In our campus planning, we began with buildings all the students visited frequently. Our goal was for students to interact more with each other, faculty, and the community.

RENOVATION OF THE BRISTER LIBRARY AND TOWER

The interior campus renovations started with the Brister Library and Tower. The library underwent extensive renovations and housed University College and Extended Programs. Subsequently, the Tower section was renovated and renamed for John Wilder, a long-time Tennessee lieutenant governor. The Tower opened in 2003 and housed campus-wide student services, admissions, financial aide, the registrar, and general academic advising, including academic services for student-athletes.

In addition, the campus master plan made changes to the center of campus, including a beautiful fountain that became a gathering spot. Similarly, the plan called for refreshing other green spaces to retain the character of the campus and make it a pleasant outdoor environment. The campus was designated a State Arboretum for the numbers and species of trees. New construction in the heart of the campus included the student activities plaza and fountain. We named a majestic clock tower and a large services building that housed the bookstore for my predecessor, V. Lane Rawlins.

THE UNIVERSITY CENTER – THE LARGEST BUILDING PROJECT IN THE HISTORY OF THE UNIVERSITY

During my secret visit to the campus just prior to my interview for president, I noted how few students were in the old university center. It was not a very appealing place, with poor lighting, inadequate ventilation, and little directional signage. A very visible meeting room used for student government (SGA) meetings looked like an elementary classroom with desks.

I scheduled one of the Board of Visitors meetings in the SGA space, believing that these key advisors and philanthropists should not just see the beautiful Holiday Inn and the futuristic FedEx Institute, but they needed to see the spaces that students used daily. When I mentioned tentative future plans to renovate the University Center, one board member said, "You have to get on this project right away, no matter what other projects you have undertaken." Even though I was still reeling from the budget freeze, reduced state appropriations, and in the process of building the FedEx Institute of Technology, I knew he was right. A poorly constructed old building with inadequate space, a damp basement, insufficient kitchen facilities, and elevators prone to stop in mid-ride was not what we wanted for our students.

After our decision was made in 2003 about the location, which was on the present site of the old student center, we secured permission from TBR and the State of Tennessee to demolish the old building and build our new dream University Center. The process took longer than expected because of declining state appropriations for higher education. With the declining revenue picture, eventually, we asked students to take on an additional $96 of debt, spread over their four years of attendance, to pay off a 30-year state school bond to finance the construction. With the funding source identified, we began construction of the University Center which would total 196,000 square feet on three levels and cost $54 million.

The new University Center opened in 2010 to rave reviews. Emblematically, it was a glorious sign that the University cared about the students, and we wanted the spaces to be beautiful and functional. The center became a prominent place on campus and in the city where students, faculty, staff, and community could interact. From the architecture community, I was given the Frances Gassner award that recognized "outstanding contributions to the quality of the built environment in Memphis," an honor I gladly shared with Tony Poteet, Assistant Vice President for Campus Planning and Design.

Impressive bronze statue of mascot Tom the Tiger unveiled in front of the new University Center.

LIVING/LEARNING COMPLEX

Another plan to create more of a sense of community among our students was the construction of the first Living/Learning Residence Complex. The concept was to form communities of students with similar majors and house them near each other. Again, from the ashes of one building another rose. We demolished West Hall to provide space to create the Living/Learning Complex.

The new residence hall was the first to be built specifically as a Living/Learning Complex. The concept was so successful that other communities formed in existing residence halls and in the Carpenter Complex adopted the model. One of the communities in the Living/Learning Complex was the honors program. We renovated space for the offices of the Helen Hardin Honors Program. Our honors program grew to be the largest in the state of Tennessee.

ICON OF THE CAMPUS: THE HOLIDAY INN

In my first year as president, the Holiday Inn was built on campus. It was a gift from the Kemmons and Dorothy Wilson Family Foundation. It became an operating Holiday Inn and housed our School of Hospitality and Resort Management.

The Holiday Inn changed our campus. It was immensely popular to members of the community and brought countless individuals and groups to our campus because of the outstanding dining and meeting spaces. In addition, the Wilson family, with Kemmons Wilson, Jr., as our liaison, appointed Tom Johnson and some of the best hotel people from the industry to manage the hotel. The Holiday Inn was awarded eight Torchbearer Awards for Guest Services and Product Excellence by the International Hospitality Group. Eventually, we added the Fogelman Executive Center across Central Avenue as part of the management of the hotel.

ICON OF THE CAMPUS: THE FEDEX INSTITUTE OF TECHNOLOGY

Shortly after my arrival on campus, Rob Carter, CIO of FedEx Corporation, and I hatched some ambitious plans, on the back of a napkin at lunch at the Grove Grill. We were keenly interested in a facility that had the potential to advance the use of technology and promote our research capabilities. We built the FedEx Institute of Technology on campus with the financial support and technical expertise of FedEx and with some funds from the State of Tennessee.

The grand celebration for the opening of the FedEx Institute of Technology.

Futuristic in design, the building included shared cutting-edge research spaces and several auditoriums. One auditorium had giant projection screens, the capability to create and project holograms, technology for language translations, televising meetings, and the security to hold high-level conferences.

We used the space and technology capabilities to interact with Nobel Laureates, government leaders, and prominent researchers from around the world. The medical device industry, economic development organizations, venture capitalists, and other future-oriented groups held meetings there.

A spin-off of the FedEx Institute of Technology was the Crews Center for Entrepreneurship, named for Hilliard and Harriett Crews. We acquired a vacant Masonic Temple near the campus and renovated it as operating space to build and commercialize prototypes.

The FedEx Institute of Technology and the Crews Center were indications that business leaders were interested in cultivating an entrepreneurial spirit throughout the university. As a result of the partnerships, I was invited to speak at the White House conference on universities' roles in driving economic development through entrepreneurship.

Iconic Building: Cecil C. Humphreys School of Law

Another iconic building project occurred when we relocated the Cecil C. Humphreys School of Law to the historic US Customs House and Post Office near the Mississippi River on Front Street. The marbled columned historic building from 1929 housed the old Customs House for river traffic on the Mississippi, the relics of several federal courts, and an official federal post office. This proposed location for our law school would provide law school students and faculty easy access to the local, state, and federal courts. Relocating the law school to the historic building downtown was lobbied for by Richard Glassman, Judge Butch Childers, and the Law Alumni Association, but the American Bar Association's threat of loss of accreditation for inadequate facilities became the determining force.

The Law School Building renovation was unveiled at a gala event.

At a critical juncture of the planning and development process, a small group of us, led by John Stokes of the BOV, flew to Washington DC to meet with the Tennessee legislative delegation, especially Senator Bill Frist, then Majority Leader. Senator Frist was instrumental in championing an agreement with the postmaster general to vacate the old building in exchange for the university providing an acceptable relocation space nearby for the post office. As a result, we raised the funds and relocated the US Post Office.

After nine years of many people not giving up on the idea, the newly renovated Law School Building opened in 2010 with a grand gala. *The PreLaw Journal* named our law school building number one in the United States. The postmaster general was reported to have said to Senator Frist and others that it made a better law school than a post office.

> *Executive leaders know that erecting buildings that outlast their lifetimes are long-term projects that require perseverance. People needing instant gratification may not be suited for this level of leadership.*

OLD LAW SCHOOL BUILDING GAINS NEW FUNCTIONS

After vacating the old Law School Building on Central Avenue, we determined that the space could be drastically renovated for other uses for the College of Communications and Fine Arts. The Martha and Robert Fogelman Collection of Contemporary Arts, donated to the University, lacked sufficient gallery space. We also needed space for student art exhibits. We turned our problem building into much-needed galleries, offices, and classroom space, as well as art labs.

ADDITIONAL COMMENTS

The overall design for the campus was a call to broader interaction with diverse groups of students and faculty, as well as an open invitation to the community to visit the campus.

The redesign of the campus sites, the erection of magnificent buildings, and the acquisition of new campuses were made possible because of the teamwork among members of the President's Council. We met together for several years on Friday afternoons to sustain our efforts. We persisted against great odds and prevailed. Working with many community, state, and national representatives, we overcame the complexities, adversities, and controversies. A genuine bond of trust, confidence, and assurance grew among us.

My belief in the people who chose to work with me and the magnificence of the ideas we generated energized and sustained me for my 12 years of service.

Chapter 11

BEYOND THE BOUNDARIES

When a university president or a company CEO decides to add locations, boards must be convinced, constituents must be supportive, and concrete plans have to be created. Moving the confines of our campus beyond Central Avenue required all those dynamics. Some moves were highly successful, but others did not have the level of success we expected.

THE MILLINGTON CAMPUS ACQUISITION AND EXPANSION

Elected officials can be of great benefit to the university by using their status to present a request or justify a proposal. U.S. Representative John Tanner was able to secure the approval of federal agencies to donate buildings on the Millington Naval Base to the university. In the fall of 2002, we acquired a dorm, Willis Hall, and a vacant six-story hospital. We were able to renovate space in Willis Hall for offices, classrooms, and the activities center that opened in 2004.

We were not able to secure additional funding from the state to renovate the hospital property, so we utilized our existing classroom renovation funds and sought donations. As a result, we received funding from Patriot Bank and a grant from BancorpSouth. We were able to renovate 40,000 square feet of the first floor of the hospital for classroom space, which opened in 2006.

As I left the presidency in 2013, I felt we had not yet captured the full possibilities of the site and the imagination of the community. They were accustomed to the naval base always being there and to multiple universities from around the nation providing classes at the site. We needed more alumni and community leadership to push the Millington campus to become a more vibrant initiative.

THE COLLIERVILLE CAMPUS

For many years, the University operated classes to serve the Collierville community in sections of the Carrier Air Conditioning Factory. Eventually, Carrier required the space back. While we were considering what alternatives we had for finding space to continue our services to the area, the City of Collierville stepped in. They were so dedicated to having University of Memphis classes there that they issued a 20-year bond, built the building, and leased it to us for $1 a year. Again, the reputation of the University and the desire for communities to have better access to higher education meant they were willing to work with the University in some creative approaches.

THE UNIVERSITY OF MEMPHIS LAMBUTH CAMPUS

Lambuth University was a small Methodist, primarily liberal arts institution, located in Jackson, Tennessee, approximately 1½ hours from Memphis. The institution fell on hard times and eventually filed for bankruptcy.

Press conference announcing the University had acquired the rights to the Lambuth University property.

At their request and with considerable support from former Lambuth alumni, U of M alumni, and community leaders, we developed a plan to take over the campus facilities and buildings after the bankruptcy proceedings were final. Lambuth University eventually closed its doors on June 30, 2011, and U of M took over the facilities and land August 8, 2011, to begin operating the fall semester with academic programs that already existed on the Memphis campus. With the full support of the Tennessee Board of Regents and the Tennessee Higher Education Commission, the records of the former Lambuth University students were archived. The Southern Association of Colleges and Schools – Commission on Colleges, worked with us to transfer students and programs and establish the Lambuth campus as a part of the University of Memphis. We were committed to providing programs the students wanted and the community needed.

On a cold winter day, January 12, 2012, Governor Bill Haslam and I hoisted the flags of the State of Tennessee and the flag with the U of M academic shield, designating the campus as the University of Memphis, Lambuth Campus.

THE COMMUNITY HEALTH BUILDING

When the need for a new community health building was presented to Governor Bredesen, we knew that we would be required to raise a certain percentage of the funds as a match to acquire state funds. Advocates and administrators met with Bredesen and told him of their hospitals' needs for nurses and the growing shortage in Memphis. An expanded program and increased enrollment could provide more graduates and more nurses for the workforce. However, our nursing program needed increased space and a new building to expand the enrollment.

Tony Poteet of Campus Planning and Design, Dean Marjorie Luttrell of Nursing, and Dean Maurice Mendel of Communication Sciences and Disorders conducted numerous visits around the nation to top-flight facilities for nursing and for communications and speech therapy. Their visits resulted in a state of the art plan for the community health building.

In 2013 before I resigned, I had the privilege of ordering 30 golden shovels for each of the 30 staunch supporters of the Community Health Building, indicating we had raised the money, designed the magnificent plans and were starting construction. On the Park Avenue Campus, we each dug up a scoop of dirt and tossed it into the air for the groundbreaking ceremony. While there were speeches and receptions, the symbolism was not lost on the magnitude of the effort to achieve the private and state funds and to be able to break ground for the Community Health Building. The new building would house our Loewenberg School of Nursing and our top-flight School of Communication Sciences and Disorders.

> *When you thank people for working on a project, give them a meaningful symbol of their partnership with you. For example, a replica of a golden shovel or a hard hat can represent their involvement with a significant building project.*

The site for the Community Health building on the Park Avenue campus held great significance. After the Kennedy Hospital for World War II soldiers was closed, the Veterans Administration gave the U of M the land in 1967. Mrs. Sally Wallace Hook was a volunteer nurse in the old Kennedy Hospital. She recalled that an oak tree was planted for every soldier who died at the hospital. Those magnificent oak trees still grew around the campus. After meeting Mrs. Hook and hearing the remembrances of others about the hospital and the World War II veterans, it became a sacred bond to me to place the Community Health Building on that site and to preserve those trees for as long as possible. As a tribute, Mrs. Hook's son, Frederick W. Smith with his family, donated funds to name the welcoming lobby and reception area in the Community Health Building in her honor.

ADDITIONAL COMMENTS:

Every decision regarding a public building on any of our campuses required deliberations involving multiple parts of the administration, state officials, and sometimes the national government. Campus master plans, political decisions, policy constraints, time, and financial limits surrounded the complicated and sometimes controversial decisions about the buildings, their locations, and always the controversy of resources.

When local officials and private influencers expressed enthusiasm for our plans, we were more successful. They were key to our success in Millington, Collierville, and in Jackson for the University of Memphis, Lambuth Campus. Trusted university officials also were keys to our success. Kevin Roper from Government Relations made certain we had the appropriate elected officials engaged with us, whether at the local, state or national levels. Among others, Dr. Dan Lattimore, Vice Provost for Extended Programs, served as the first campus dean for U of M Lambuth and worked with communities, including elected officials for the Millington and Collierville expansions. The views of alumni, donors, school boards, corporate executives, community leaders, state legislators, and both Chancellor Charles Manning and later Chancellor John Morgan influenced public opinion and made it possible for us to acquire private support and public funds to make each move.

As complicated as it may seem, the university president is only one part of the puzzle to begin and execute building plans, acquire land, and marshal the needed resources. The President's Council, acting as the leadership team, supplied the expertise, skills, political insights, and knowledge of state and private funding arrangements that made it possible for us to carry out our bold plans.

Chapter 12:

ATHLETICS IN PERSPECTIVE

The University of Memphis competes in NCAA Division 1 athletics. During my presidency, we granted athletic scholarships in 18 sports, nine for men and nine for women. Men's basketball and football games had the largest following. As a matter of fact, U of M athletic competitions attracted the largest attendance of any events in the city.

The popularity of athletics was a huge benefit to the university in many ways, including media attention and revenue. On the downside, many other important stories about the university were downplayed or outright lost. For example, U of M had highly ranked academic programs in every college, award-winning leadership initiatives in student affairs, breakthroughs in research, and life-changing community involvement. Yet, athletic competitions, particularly in basketball and football, captured the media's attention.

For me as president, it was a balancing act. I recognized that Tiger Athletics was a source of civic and campus pride. Whether it was the entertainment value, flamboyant nature of the coaches, or the need to associate with winners, the members of the public identified themselves as "Tigers," even if they had not graduated from the university. They supported the Memphis Tigers because they lived in the city that bore our name. While the president and the administrative leaders enjoyed the athletic spectacles and successes, athletes and athletic competitions must be integrated into the overall university culture. Keep in mind that student-athletes are students first.

LEARNING HOW TO HANDLE A HOT POTATO

Shortly after I was selected U of M president, the men's basketball team was playing in a conference tournament in Louisville. Even though I was not scheduled to arrive on campus and assume the full reins of the job until July 1, Bob and I decided to attend the tournament.

A bevy of sports reporters covering the tournament greeted us. One of the questions they asked me was whether or not I would keep R.C. Johnson as the athletics director. In fact, R.C. and I had just met for the first time. I quickly answered that I would be meeting with the senior leadership team at the university and discussing the team members' future plans as soon as I arrived on campus in about six months. Somehow the media interpreted my statement as less than a resounding endorsement of the current A.D. and generated news reports to that end. That exchange with the media was a clear indicator to me that I was a novice at impromptu press conferences.

Given the media's interest in our A.D.'s future, my decision could not wait for six months. I contacted people I knew in the athletics world, including the University of Kentucky's athletic director,

C.M. Newton, and scheduled a meeting with Mr. Johnson the very next day. After an engaging and productive session, I asked R.C. to continue as the athletics director and made that announcement public through the U of M sports information di-

As the senior executive, recognize your limitations and get specialized training or hire consultants who can help you acquire the skills to work in any area of need. Acquiring communications skills to work with the media is imperative for most CEO's. Do not procrastinate on needed training.

rector. With that settled, the reporters returned to covering the tournament and our celebrity coach John Calipari, whom I did not meet until weeks later at a reception on campus.

For me, lesson learned.

The University of Memphis Athletics Director

The early decision about Mr. Johnson was a significant one. He had a great personality, vast knowledge of sports, and quick wit. He connected well with audiences and donors. During our 11 years of working together, he and I met at least once a week about a news story, student issue, coach's concern, question from the conference, or media request. He also routinely met with the President's Council. Across the country, most athletic directors were not involved with leaders at the senior administrative level.

R.C. was highly regarded among athletics directors throughout the NCAA. They were envious of the fundraising infrastructure he had built through the Ambassador's Club for major donors and the Tiger Scholarship Clubs. As an indication of their esteem, Johnson was elected by his peers to the Leadership Council of the NCAA.

DEALING WITH CELEBRITY

One of the most famous coaches in U of M history was John Calipari. Mr. Johnson hired Coach Calipari in 2000, one year before I arrived. When the Tigers began winning conference tournaments and getting bids to compete in the NCAA Tournament, John won over the fans. Known as a great recruiter and coach, Calipari proved it by winning 214 games in his nine years at Memphis, more than Coach Larry Finch, U of M's winningest coach until Calipari arrived.

Coach Calipari was selected as a 2015 inductee into the Basketball Hall of Fame. In a radio interview prior to the induction ceremony, R.C. Johnson was interviewed about Coach Calipari and his selection. R.C. described John affectionately as a hustler and entrepreneur who is gregarious, intense, and high-profile. I concurred with that description.

Our coach had gained notoriety for his confrontations with sports reporters when they questioned him or the team, but he was engaging in his responses. If he was not making news locally, he was in demand by ESPN and other national sports outlets. He had been in the national spotlight so often that he was almost as comfortable there as he was on the basketball court. He did not hesitate to say what he thought, good or bad, controversial or flattering.

Without a doubt, Coach Calipari raised the caliber of basketball played in Memphis, and he raised money for the athletics department by putting fans in the stands and becoming friends with prominent donors. He gave philanthropically to the community privately and publicly, including donations to the University. And, he increased the graduation rates of players, nearing 80%, before he left for the University of Kentucky.

Over the nine years he was with the University of Memphis, he showed compassion for many people. I personally know of numerous incidences when John called people who were ill, visited patients in hospitals, and supported people behind the scenes. He was public in his support of Ken Bennett and the Street Ministries who worked with inner-city youth. He was a champion in basketball, always a magnet for a media frenzy, and a handful for the athletic director and the president.

2008 BASKETBALL SEASON: A PIVOTAL ONE

In 2008, Memphis men's basketball achieved a 38-game winning streak, the longest in NCAA history, and gained a number-one ranking. National media clamored for coverage. The swelling civic pride in Memphis was palpable. 2008 would be only the second time we had competed in the national championship game.

Unfortunately, we lost the championship game to the Kansas Jayhawks in overtime, but that loss was not the final blow. Coach Calipari had reached such prominence that he was being heavily recruited by a national basketball powerhouse, the University of Kentucky. And, our athletic program was facing allegations that the SAT score of one of our basketball players was questionable.

The facts seemed straightforward and easily resolvable. But that proved not to be true. The allegations were based on information from the Educational Testing Service (ETS) that one of our players had not acknowledged correspondence from them asking questions about his SAT test scores. The correspondence had been sent to the player at his home address, where he no longer resided. Without a response from the player, the ETS questions went unanswered. The administration learned about the issue only after the

NCAA Infractions Committee notice arrived. Meanwhile, the player claimed he took the test, and the coach said he had no information about the test score.

As a penalty, 38 wins for that season were vacated by the NCAA. Even worse, the integrity of the university was called into question.

I headed a delegation to the ETS headquarters in Princeton, New Jersey, and met with the executive director. We asked him to work with his board and reconsider the policy and procedure of only notifying the student concerning questions. We asked them to notify the university as soon as any questions about scores arise. I sent information about our meeting with ETS to the presidents in the C-USA conference, to those serving with me on the NCAA Board and to the Executive Committee. To my knowledge, ETS has not changed their policy and continues to keep all correspondence between the organization and the student, which leaves universities in jeopardy.

Meanwhile, Coach Calipari accepted Kentucky's offer and departed for Lexington. His tenure at Memphis had resulted in nine consecutive 20-win seasons and four consecutive 30-win seasons, endearing him to Memphis fans. His success was widely heralded, but a lot of stalwart Tigers fans could not forgive him for leaving Memphis for Kentucky with some of our players and many of the coaching staff.

COACHING CHANGES ARE PART OF THE JOB DESCRIPTION

After Coach Calipari left for Kentucky in 2009, the next major basketball question concerned his replacement. I supported R.C.'s decision that Josh Pastner become our new coach. Josh was a young assistant coach under Calipari and had been an assistant at the University of Arizona. He had worked in winning programs. Josh,

31 at the time, was clean cut and had a positive attitude, basketball savvy, and the ability to recruit good players.

After Josh was appointed, I explicitly stated three demands for him to follow with respect to student athletes. Do not break NCAA rules and policies. Make sure players follow the rules and stay out of trouble with the law. Work to make sure that all players attend classes regularly, make academic gains, and graduate. From the 2009 season until I left in 2013, Coach Pastner met those demands, and players who stayed for four years had a 100% graduation rate. Josh also took the team to NCAA tournaments four times.

FOOTBALL PROBLEMS IN MEMPHIS

Football is always a lightning rod for media and fan attention, for better or for worse. Tommy West was football coach for nine years and took the team to five bowl games. The Tiger football team had been to only one other bowl in the history of the program. However, in 2009 with a decreasing number of wins and declining fan attendance, Coach West was dismissed.

During his last interview as head coach, he said emphatically that for Tiger football to be more successful, a more positive emphasis on football was needed from the media, the fans, and the administration. Rest assured that my administration wanted success for the football program. We knew that the program needed some upgrades, including better practice facilities, weight rooms, a turf field, and upgrades for an indoor practice facility. However, all of these improvements required substantial funds that were dependent on fan attendance at games and dedicated donors.

Coaching Search. Struggling to take the next steps for the football program, Athletic Director Johnson appointed Larry Porter as coach. Porter was a former Memphis Tigers running back who had won recruiting awards on the coaching staff at Louisiana State University. He was not successful. He stayed two years and only won three games. He was dismissed in 2011.

The football program was in a tailspin. The situation was difficult for Tiger Football, for the U of M Athletics department, and for our dwindling but loyal fans. Then, Athletics Director Johnson announced in 2011 that he would retire on June 30, 2012. He had served for nearly 16 years at the University of Memphis, ending a career of 32 years in athletics director positions and ten years as a coach at other universities.

Without an A.D., finding a new head football coach became my responsibility. Because of the timing of the season for recruiting players, we needed to hire a new head football coach before we could attract a new A.D., not the preferred sequence. On November 28, 2011, I announced the steps for the football coach search in a memo to the university and community.

While recruiting and hiring coaches is usually a more private process, I decided to use another approach. The steps were to secure the services of the Eastman-Beaudine firm that specialized in athletics searches. In addition, I appointed a search committee co-chaired by Brad Martin, chairman of the Board of Visitors, and Willie Gregory, director of Community

Taking a different tactic is often needed. Do not be bound by the 'we've always done it this way' approach. You are in charge. Take charge and make changes.

and Business Relations for Nike operations in Memphis. I also appointed Mike Fredi, president of the Highland Hundred Fan Club; Cato Johnson from the Alumni Association; Tom Watson from the

Ambassadors; Alan Graf, president of the Tiger Athletics Board; Dr. Ed Stevens, a professor who also served as the faculty representative to Athletics; as well as Sheryl Lipman, university legal counsel. While not the usual process for coaching appointments, I also announced that basically we would follow the same process for selecting the next A.D. Much like selecting other leaders of the university, we would proceed with broad participation.

The search process led us to Justin Fuente from Texas Christian University (TCU), who was an offensive coordinator when they won the Rose Bowl. We interviewed finalists in New York, where coaches were gathered for a conference. We had been disappointed in the coaching candidates' lack of enthusiasm for our program. Who could blame them with our losing record over the last two years, the lowest ranked defensive team in the country, and dwindling attendance at football games?

Coach Fuente arrived, barely making the interview in time because of heavy New York traffic, and our outlook became more favorable. He came with a written plan for developing champions and equated us with TCU in previous years. His knowledge and reputation were solid. Fuente also had researched the university and our leadership team, and he seemed undaunted by the prospect of accepting his first head coach job without knowing who the A.D. would be. If we chose him, Justin would be another young coach,

Employ someone who really wants the position you have to offer, not someone you have to convince to take it.

only 36 years old. Flying back home to Memphis, we knew he was the one. We did our research by interviewing his TCU head coach and other references. We liked his style of play and coaching. We decided he would be a good match for U of M. He was.

Fuente coached football at Memphis for three seasons, won coaching awards, had players who were named All-Americans, took our team to bowl games, and recruited brilliantly, especially in attracting a star quarterback. I was confident that the football program was in good hands with Justin Fuente. However, we still had to find an athletics director.

Athletics Director Search. We followed the same process in our A.D. search as we had for a coach. In the meetings with candidates, I questioned them vigorously about their fundraising abilities, engagement with fans, and process for integrating athletics into the overall university. In the end, we hired Tom Bowen, A.D. at San Jose State University in California.

To introduce Tom Bowen as the new athletics director, R.C. Johnson presided over the press conference and proclaimed his classic line, "It's another great day to be a Tiger." Bowen began as A.D. on June 30, 2012, R.C.'s last day.

Bowen reorganized much of the Athletic department's operations in fundraising and ticketing, as well as several managerial positions. He met with coaches of all the sports, fan clubs, and donors. Tom readily made public appearances and soon learned to deal with the intense scrutiny of the Memphis media.

SENIOR WOMEN'S ATHLETICS DIRECTOR

Lynn Parkes was on the staff of the University of Memphis for 38 years. She came to U of M to start the golf program and then became the senior women's administrator and eventually assistant athletic director. She also worked on NCAA compliance for all the sports and served on several NCAA committees over her career.

The women's coaches reported to Ms. Parkes. In the past, Lynn had worked with multiple sports, including volleyball, women's golf, men's and women's track, and women's tennis.

Ms. Parkes was especially helpful to me in reviewing Title IX requirements and starting the softball program. Bob and I have many great experiences with women's sports, particularly basketball, soccer, volleyball, and softball. We admired the women and their coaches in tennis, golf, track and field, and rifle. The media attention remained with women's basketball.

I also admired Ms. Elma Roane, a pioneer women's basketball coach who was recognized for her advocacy for women's sports, and for whom the fieldhouse was named. The elderly Ms. Roane, now deceased, never hesitated to give advice about athletics. I am a strong believer in Title IX and in the values of competition, team play, sense of accomplishment, and the spirit of camaraderie that sports engender. I felt numerous conflicts about the funding of sports for male athletes versus those for women.

WOMEN'S BASKETBALL

Women's basketball received the most attention among the women's sports. However, soccer and volleyball were gaining momentum as their programs excelled and recruited some top-quality athletes. Watching the team play in Roane Fieldhouse, with the Pep Band playing and the enthusiastic cheerleaders pumping out familiar cheers and chants was exhilarating. Many fans were former women's players, high school athletes, or members of other sports teams. The parking was free, the snacks affordable, and the fans familiar. The experience was worthwhile, even with a hardback or no back seat, and a crackly sound system. It was hardly comparable to the professional team status of the FedEx Forum where the men played their games. For the few games the women played there, the crowd seemed too small and spread out, but the enthusiastic fan base remained the same whatever the venue.

Joye Lee-McNelis was the women's basketball coach when I arrived in 2001. After being at U of M for 13 years with two NCAA tournament appearances and three in the Women's National Invitation Tournament (WNIT), she departed for Southern Mississippi in 2003 to be near her family. The coach who followed her stayed four years without any winning seasons and was replaced.

In 2008, Lynn Parkes and R.C. Johnson recruited Melissa McFerrin. She coached the Tigers in C-USA with winning seasons in four out of five years until Memphis joined the American Athletic Conference where the competition was stiffer.

COMMENTS ABOUT OTHER SPORTS

Other sports received far less attention than football and men's and women's basketball. However, all of the teams had an enthusiastic fan base, particularly baseball. We also had men's teams in golf, tennis, track and field, and rifle. We had women's teams in softball, volleyball, golf, tennis, track and field, and mixed teams in rifle.

During my time at Memphis, I interacted with the sports teams by attending games in baseball, basketball, softball, volleyball, and soccer. For many of the awards events at the end of the season, I interacted with the coaches and various student-athletes. I learned about them as individuals, not just athletes. I felt immensely proud of them for their accomplishments, but I also appreciated their personalities and goodwill that made them such good team players.

These athletes often expressed their gratitude for their scholarships, academic support, and always spoke about their relationships with their coaches.

ATHLETICS FACILITIES

On a college campus, design and construction of athletic facilities are major parts of the campus master plan. Because of fans' attendance at competitions, athletic facilities are often the most visible buildings to the community. Athletics Director R.C. Johnson, the consummate fundraiser for athletics, spearheaded many highly successful campaigns for building and renovating facilities.

During Mr. Johnson's tenure, numerous facilities were built on the Park Avenue Campus, including the FedEx Field for baseball, the Frank Flautt Golf Center, and the women's softball field. New tennis facilities were secured at the Racquet Club. On the main campus, renovations were made to the Elma Roane Fieldhouse for women's basketball and volleyball, the Finch Center basketball practice complex, and the Anfernee "Penny" Hardaway Hall of Fame—the headquarters for the Athletics department. Johnson also worked with the county to operate the Mike Rose Soccer Complex; the Pyramid, that served as the home court for men's basketball until the FedEx Forum was opened; and with the Liberty Bowl Memorial Stadium, the home field for football.

CONTROVERSIES OVER THE PYRAMID AND THE LIBERTY BOWL

Controversies swirled around both the Pyramid and the Liberty Bowl that involved me as president. In the early years of my tenure, the City of Memphis was actively recruiting a professional basketball team, eventually landing the Memphis Grizzlies. The Grizzlies Organization decided the Pyramid, the home of the Tigers, was inadequate for a pro team.

Pyramid or FedEx Forum. As a part of the deal for the Grizzlies to move to Memphis, the City of Memphis decided to construct a new arena. With the need for local tax funds to be used, a heated debate ensued. The University was involved because the question became whether the Memphis Tigers would leave the Pyramid or move to the new arena to be constructed. Calls came to my office from politicians, reporters, columnists, and donors about these two facilities. Major donors and foundations let me know that they were interested in us moving to the arena that would eventually be named the FedEx Forum.

The Pyramid had opened in 1991 and was owned originally by both the city and the county, but in 2009 the county sold its share to the city. Until the Grizzlies came to town, the Memphis Tigers men's basketball team was the major tenant for the Pyramid. Many citizens felt if we moved our game venue, the Pyramid, like the Mid-South Coliseum before it, would become just another vacant sports structure. Some prominent politicians, state legislators, and local citizens were against spending more tax revenue on sports venues. The mayor and some city council members decided to support the building and operation of the arena with tax revenues.

To make our decision about whether to stay at the Pyramid or leave for the FedEx Forum, we needed more information. Cost analyses revealed that we could not support the operation of the Pyramid solely on Tiger Basketball revenue and that sharing an arena, the new FedEx Forum, was our best financial move. We made our case with the Tennessee Board of Regents and received permission to play our games in the FedEx Forum. The compromise stipulation from TBR was that we not serve alcoholic beverages or share in proceeds from any liquor sales in the FedEx Forum.

Armed with facts, opinions of donors, input of citizens and students, regulatory bodies, and the media, it remains the leader's responsibility to make the decisions and negotiate any compromises that address the needs and the integrity of the organization.

Liberty Bowl Memorial Stadium. The university and the city had a long-standing relationship with respect to the operation of the stadium that opened in 1965 with a seating capacity of about 60,000. It was built with the intent of attracting a permanent professional football team to Memphis. That goal was never realized, but various football and soccer teams had short lives there.

The regular games played at the Liberty Bowl were Tiger football home games and the Southern Heritage Classic between Jackson State in Mississippi and Tennessee State - two HBCUs, historically Black colleges and universities. At the end of the football season, the Autozone Liberty Bowl game is played there as one of the national bowl games. Through the years, the Memphis Tigers football team was the Liberty Bowl Memorial Stadium's major tenant.

The stadium had numerous problems and needed to be renovated. Some old fairgrounds properties adjacent to the stadium were eyesores and due to be torn down.

Newly elected Memphis Mayor A C Wharton, in cooperation with Steve Ehrhart, executive director of the Autozone Liberty Bowl, authorized the architectural drawings of plans for renovations of the stadium and surrounding grounds. Because the old Mid-South Fairgrounds were vacant, dilapidated barns in the neglected area around the stadium were demolished without controversy.

Eventually, the site was beautifully renovated with the addition of an attractive new tower, as well as a fountain and blue lighting to enhance the main entrance. Tiger Lane was established for parking and tailgating, designating the Liberty Bowl Stadium as the home of the Memphis Tigers football team.

Despite the positive plans, before they could be carried out, a local sports commentator and some sports enthusiasts proposed that the University construct a new university-financed on-campus stadium, rather than share in the renovation costs of the existing Liberty Bowl stadium.

This issue pitted me against some good friends among the fans and alumni. By looking at what other universities were building, I did not think it made sense for the university to build an on-campus stadium when we had one less than two miles away. In addition, I could not find a single major donor willing to contribute to building a new stadium. The emphatic "no's" from potential contributors was no surprise when we realized they or their families had been some of the original donors who financed the construction of the Liberty Bowl Memorial Stadium in the 1960s.

The commentator and some of the most ardent fans had made their public stance. While I was away at a meeting in Nashville, I called in a quote to our communications director. In effect, the message was to the news media that I did not think it was in the best interest of the university to build an on-campus stadium because of financial constraints and space limitations on campus. That quote raised the ire of the commentator and his supporters.

After much wrangling over an on-campus stadium versus renovations to the Liberty Bowl Stadium, I agreed for Mr. Johnson to appoint a committee of Board of Visitors members and several ardent fans to explore the matter. The committee recommended that the university not build an on-campus stadium. No donors I could locate were willing to contribute the millions of dollars that would be necessary to build an on-campus stadium. Finally, the state offered no support.

Fortunately, the public outcry for an on-campus stadium diminished when the renovations of the Liberty Bowl Stadium actually began. Aware of plans for a new giant scoreboard, seat backs in the stands, and constructing Tiger Lane, people were eager to see if we could deliver on the university partnership with the city-owned Liberty Bowl.

It was a thrill at the first football game when we opened Tiger Lane to our fans who tailgated there with their tents arrayed near the fountain. Memphis' famous barbeque smells filled the air. The expansive green space hosted fans and children tossing footballs. Memphis music rocked from the alumni tent, only to be interrupted by the Mighty Sound of the South marching band. The band announced the arrival of Coach Fuente, who led his players through cheering crowds. I was delighted with the results and marveled at the attractive grounds outside the stadium where old dilapidated fairgrounds barns once stood.

Fans on Tiger Lane awaiting the team's march through the crowd on their way to Liberty Bowl Memorial Stadium.

CONFERENCE REALIGNMENT

In athletics, ambition and change are expected. The University of Memphis athletics program felt the pull of bigger and better conference alignment. When I arrived in 2001, we were members of C-USA. In 2012, U of M joined the Big East Conference, and in that same year, the conference morphed into a newly formed American Athletic Conference (AAC), leaving behind the basketball only schools.

Soon after my appointment as president of U of M, I was asked to serve as chair of C-USA, the first woman to hold the position and was elected for a second term. Also, I was selected as the conference's representative to the NCAA Board of Directors to replace the Tulane president who dropped out to deal with the aftermath of Hurricane Katrina. I was appointed to the NCAA executive committee and then was elected by C-USA to continue as its NCAA representative for a second term. At that time, I was the only woman on the NCAA board and executive committee. Needless to say, from the NCAA meetings in Indianapolis, I learned a great deal about the layers of policies affecting student-athletes, athletics directors, conferences, officiating, and revenue streams.

All university presidents are highly engaged in decisions about the operations of the athletic program, whatever the level. However, Division 1 decisions carry a responsibility that consumes a great deal of time, much data analysis, media attention, and a clear need to keep the focus on the student athlete. The athletic program, A.D., and coaches are the topics of conversations and headlines around the conference, on TV sports networks, and locally, wanted or not.

Promise versus Reality

In a sports-minded city like Memphis, on a campus that was accustomed to national prominence in basketball, and recent success in football, other sports received far less attention. As the University president, I followed the win-loss records of the teams intently, but I also was concerned about the coaches' treatments of the student athletes, their academic achievements, and the teams' responsiveness to the fans and the community.

At the University of Kentucky, as a dean and as vice chancellor for academic services, athletic academic advising was one of my responsibilities. I had learned to look at the quality of tutoring, facilities, and engagement of athletes with the rest of the university. Unfortunately, upon my arrival at the University of Memphis, I found some qualified tutors, but not the number and engagement with faculty I expected, nor the time and attention student athletes needed.

We made improvements. We moved the athletic advising and academic center to the newly renovated Wilder Tower with other student services. We employed Dr. Joe Luckey as Director of Athletic Academics to restructure the Center for Athletic Academic Services. He became a respected member of the Provost's staff, which was the reporting structure I required. He also reported to the A.D. with the expectation that he would keep the A.D. informed of how each team was performing academically.

Dr. Luckey also reviewed the NCAA eligibility of each player and worked with the team's staff members who were responsible for the academic progress rate (APR) for each team. He added the life-skills training that helped athletes deal with their personal needs.

In his ten years, all of our athletic teams achieved NCAA-APR, academic progress rate, standards. I firmly believe that the partnership between the offices of Provost Ralph Faudree and Joe Luckey made our academic athletics program successful and nationally recognized. A.D. Johnson and I had fewer worries about whether we were providing what our student athletes needed to be successful both as students and athletes. In many ways, the academic services that worked for student-athletes also proved helpful for non-athletes.

While many universities, including Memphis, had well-publicized incidences of players in trouble with the law, the majority excelled in their sports, met academic standards, participated in community projects, and individually reached out to fans, particularly children. With few exceptions, the coach sets the standard. Our basketball and football players were often in the limelight and dealt with excessive expectations. We counseled them and helped them develop in healthy ways as young men and women. We wanted them to grow to be responsible adults and to represent the university, their families, and themselves well. We helped them build their own reputations as well-educated, respectable individuals, not just athletes.

I am and have always been a fan, but I learned first-hand about the extraordinarily difficult circumstances many of our players endured as children and the increased scrutiny placed on them. I realized that sports made a significant difference in their lives. Individual and team successes built the student-athletes' confidence and self-esteem. I enjoyed watching them perform and respected their efforts to bring home a win. I never lost sight of the fact that foremost they were students who were learning skills and tapping into the knowledge a college education can provide. I had high expectations for them as students and even higher expectations for our coaches and athletic director.

ADDITIONAL COMMENTS

Athletics remains the cheerleader for the university, but the president has the responsibility to remind the teams that they represent the university. While I found myself spending much more time with athletic activities than I had ever imagined, these responsibilities focused my attention on the values of the university. I believe that most university athletic directors, coaches, and players enter their sports with high ideals. I also believe that too many young athletes experience undue pressure from family members, have to fend off scouts and agents from the professional ranks, and live with unfair assessments of their strengths and weaknesses. Many experienced pitfalls developing themselves as professionals in other fields, leaving far too many in jeopardy when their reliance had been so great on sports. I like this motto from a former NCAA publicity campaign: "Most of our student athletes are preparing for careers, other than in sports."

At an NCAA conference for officers of student-athlete councils, I was asked to deliver a keynote address and advise them on turning their athletic prowess and participation on teams into leadership skills. The speech was well-received. I came back to Memphis and asked some of our financial institutions to provide training for student-athletes on financial matters. Many from poor backgrounds were concerned about making a living outside of the sports spotlight.

Chapter 13

SAYING "GOODBYE" IS HARDER THAN SAYING "HELLO"

My belief in the power of education to change lives has been the driving force throughout my career journey. Education transformed my life. My curiosity and desire to learn and understand more sustained me.

Leaving jobs along my career path meant saying goodbye to people with whom I felt deep bonds. I always appreciated the success we had together and lamented when we fell short. I was thankful for our journey together. I am eternally grateful for the camaraderie of team members who shouldered responsibilities at my requests. Leaving meant losing contact with many of these enthusiastic people, some with quirky idiosyncrasies, most with genuine goodwill, and nearly all committed to the same passion for education.

Educating young children started my career journey, and I never lost the joy of being with them. Here I am singing with the children at Campus School.

As a reflective professional and personal soul-searcher, I learned a great deal about myself over the years. I remained a determined person as I moved from one position to the next. Even with setbacks and periods of slow or no progress, the one calling that remained constant was my dedication to the cause of education. In our country, believing in the value of education is expected, but working to improve ways to communicate knowledge and critical and creative thinking skills is a grander goal. Some who espouse the goals of education become weary of trying to make changes to improve it. I was fortunate in my career to find determined kindred spirits who lived their beliefs.

MOTIVATIONS FOR CHANGE

In the previous chapters, I have discussed the processes and dilemmas of professional changes, the accompanying motivations, and my feelings. Because this is a book of leadership stories and lessons captured through my memories, I want to be honest in saying that as noble as the goals of improving education are, I sometimes made changes for other reasons.

I often moved to a new setting for more excitement, more challenges, and different people. Earlier in the book, I told the story of my farmer father who had one job all of his life. Dad said to me, "Why are you moving again? Can't you keep a job?" On the other hand, my mother, a farmer's wife, was more adventurous; she had held many jobs to support the family farm, so she always encouraged me to try different job experiences.

Moving from teaching children to leading the Head Start Program in Knoxville was an exciting time for me. It offered me an opportunity to learn more and exercise my leadership abilities for the first time in the world of education. When I left the Head Start directorship for graduate school, I experienced feelings of uncertainty because I was unemployed for a time and had just gone through a divorce. Growing up with humble means, I felt very insecure without a paycheck. To pay the bills during my graduate school days, I launched the Community Child Center at Roane State Community College in Harriman and also taught some classes there.

I acted against the advice of my graduate advisors who told me I should be a full-time student, not start a new program in a new location, get it funded, train people

You will always have doubts. As you progress in your career and try to decide what to do next, you will not always know with certainty what the best path is. You must carefully consider the options. Ask trusted colleagues for their opinions and recommendations. But, this much is true, what you think and what you want are what matter. Just because something has seldom or never been done does not mean it can't or won't be done. Go ahead, try!

and add to my responsibilities. Regardless of their advice, changing from a part-time student to a full-time student with no financial support was far riskier than I could stomach, riskier than starting a program for children, something I knew how to do. My deepest fear was that I would not be able to provide for me, my son, and later a larger family, which included my parents as they aged. My motives also included the adventures of a new place, a new challenge, and after graduate school, a new beginning.

Later when I remarried, changing locations became more challenging. It was daunting to find two positions, carve out my career, and establish my specialties and areas of expertise in research. The move from graduate school in Tennessee to university teaching in another state and administrative jobs around the Southeast left me with both a growing sense of confidence and the unanswered question as I began each new job, "Am I up to the challenge?"

Perhaps the most soul-searching change came from leaving a position I really enjoyed working at a university in the Southeast. My colleagues were terrific, but my supervisor was a problem. Leaving a difficult situation felt like running away. Fortunately, the next position was even more interesting and compelling. I did run away, but I found a more personally satisfying and professionally challenging role.

Over the years I've helped others grapple with similar questions for their careers and families. For people wanting to escape a difficult supervisor, my advice has always been that they should be certain they are running to something better. I also understood people's needs to test themselves against new challenges with new colleagues and supervisors.

My Greatest Challenge – The University of Memphis

The most daunting and the most expansive position in which I served was president of the University of Memphis. After 12 years, saying "goodbye" to the University of Memphis and the community was certainly far more difficult than saying "hello." Every year, I had become accustomed to saying "hello" to new students, new faculty, new administrators, new donors, and new community leaders.

While the challenges in leading a public research university were great because of funding and political constraints, my team and I found ways to craft effective programs, instill a sense of appreciation of people, and pay attention to the quality of our work. But it is the people, always the people, the faculty members, staff, and students that kept me going. As important as every donor or every elected official was, our team always kept the focus where it should be—on the students, their programs, and the people who could make the most difference in their lives.

Speaking at an alumni event about students making a difference on campus, in the community, and beyond.

In some ways, being a university president was a selfish endeavor for me. It fed my fascination with various fields of study and with the faculty members in each area. Their expertise and creativity were expressed in vastly different ways, depending on the area of study. I savored the lectures and looked forward to the humanities series, the great conversations events, the originality of the art exhibits, entertaining concerts, and brilliantly choreographed dance and theatre productions.

All of these special endeavors went beyond basic classroom instruction, and they were intriguing, fun, and thought-provoking. The variety of the experiences made the university environment lively and always engaging to be with students. While we helped thousands of courageous students in my days, I learned about real courage when I met the Memphis State Eight.

THE MEMPHIS STATE EIGHT HISTORICAL MARKER

As a part of the 100th anniversary of the university, we wanted to celebrate eight courageous African-American students who integrated the university in 1959. I met all eight at several events, but the unveiling of the historical marker outside the Administration Building meant the most to them and to me. Dr. Rosie Phillips Bingham and I hosted a celebration arranged by Mr. Mark Stansbury. Students, staff, faculty, administrators, families, and friends gathered for the unveiling of the historic marker. We commemorated their courage, determination, and spirit by recording oral histories and interviewing them for campus and community media outlets. They told of their fears and their determination as well as pride in paving the way for future generations. The marker reads:

"In the fall of 1959 some 4,500 students enrolled at Memphis State University. Among them were eight African Americans, the first to break the University's color barrier. They were Bertha Mae Rogers (Looney), Rose Blakney (Love), and Marvis Kneeland (Jones), graduates of Hamilton High School; Luther McClelland and John Simpson from Manassas High School; Ralph Prater and Eleanor Gandy from Douglass High School; and Sammie Burnett (Johnson) from Booker T. Washington High School. They became known as the Memphis State Eight. Once on campus they were asked to avoid the cafeteria and student center. They were barred from taking physical education classes and ROTC. Police escorted them to their classes, which were scheduled for morning. They were required to leave the campus by noon. The University set aside special restrooms and lounges for them. Unlike other schools, the Memphis State Eight met with no physical violence. They were taunted by hecklers carrying Confederate flags. . . In 2009 the University presented the Memphis State eight with the Arthur S. Holman Lifetime Achievement Award."

The men and women of the Memphis State Eight mentioned on the historical marker and commemorated for their courage for integrating the campus in 1959.

A Learning Culture throughout the Campus

One of my greatest joys as an administrator stemmed from each division embracing the requests from the President's Council to make their divisions and departments learning environments. It was exhilerating to meet with the leadership teams, as well as the vice presidents and directors associated with each division. Each team presented their plans to emphasize learning, conduct new training, study exemplary practices elsewhere, research their own effectiveness, solicit bottom-up suggestions, and vet their new understandings collectively. After hearing these learning plans, I knew my leadership team and I had established a new "learning culture."

During my time at the University of Memphis, the President's Council, my husband Bob, and I were continuous learners. We were amazed by the lives and influence of Nobel Laureates, business tycoons, struggling entrepreneurs, distinguished civil rights leaders, and researchers with simple and elegant ideas. We also learned from poor, sometimes exhausted neighborhood workers who never gave up on making life better for their communities. My team and I learned about local, state, and national initiatives from elected officials and resolute citizens who championed great causes.

Politically, we learned how to stack audiences with cheerleaders for the University District proposals to be decided by the City Council or the County Commission. We learned better communication strategies after experiencing the perils and pitfalls in keeping the state legislators, governor, and state agencies informed. Sometimes our greatest lessons came from losses and mistakes, but we did learn together.

During extremely difficult situations, I knew to retreat to my back office and to never let anyone at the university see me cry. I learned to recall Bible verses, embraced inspirational mottos, and read long philosophical pieces to stay inspired to keep going. I experienced and responded to devastating events, such as 9/11, the students from New Orleans we took in after Hurricane Katrina, the deaths of students and of beloved faculty members, and tragic accidents. Always, there were the unexpected events that shaped the campus or the myriad of unforeseen problems that needed untangling. As the symbol and human face of the university, I attended and spoke at far more funerals, wakes, and memorials than I had ever imagined I would.

I worked on communications almost constantly. Even when I wanted to take our critics head-on, I was expected to remain calm. And for the most part, I did. I listened to the university counsel and communications director, who strongly advised me to respond to critics with restraint.

I enjoyed the laughter and the fun that happened every day on the university campus. I savored each celebration for its significance to the participants. Because the university had between 22,000 and 23,000 students, thousands of alumni and community supporters, and between 2,400 and 2,500 employees, there were hundreds of celebration events, as well as athletic, academic, and creative competitions.

When awards were given out to students, faculty, and the university, I received far too much credit, but I knew that I was the symbol of the university and that the next president would become the next symbol. Unfortunately, when the athletic teams were not winning, when tuition was increased because of shortfalls in state revenue, or when a decision went counter to public opinion, I had to shoulder the blame. The person who holds the highest office is the university's symbol, the one that some people applaud and others blame. It's a hard lesson for a leader to learn, regardless of the circumstances. Certainly, the satisfaction, fun, and sheer joy I had during my 12 years were worth any blame I had to take. A leader needs considerable spiritual and emotional strength to weather the work and stay true to the values, the causes, and the great expectations of the university. Most importantly, a leader in a university should remain dedicated to learning.

CELEBRATING THE 100TH ANNIVERSARY, FUNDRAISING, AND MY GOODBYE PARTY

People in Memphis know how to party, and party we did to launch the university's 100th anniversary in 2012. At the end of the year, we used the anniversary as the culmination of our first-ever, campus-wide capital campaign and combined the end celebration as my goodbye party.

Julie Johnson, our vice president for development, and a team of dedicated community leaders launched a university-wide capital campaign. Charles Burkett, chairman of the Board of Visitors, and his wife Judy chaired the campaign. Charles and I made countless visits to major donors, wrote proposals to foundations, identified new prospects, and expressed our profound appreciation to donors for their past contributions. We always tailored our specific requests based on the donors' interests. At the end of the campaign, we had pledges and contributions of $256 million.

From the beginning of 2012, the year of our 100th anniversary, we hosted great events. Each college planned something special. The College of Education launched new awards to give to distinguished alums. The College of Engineering held events that focused on several of its centers and institutes, such as the Intermodal Freight Transportation Center and the Center for Earthquake Research and Information. The College of Business and Economics had alums teach in every class on a special day capped off with distinguished speakers. Many student groups became more involved in community events, such as teaching children to swim, collecting donations for food banks, and packing meals for the elderly.

We also celebrated the anniversary famously with music. At the beginning of the academic year, in September, Maestro Pu-Qi Jiang conducted the University of Memphis Orchestra in an original composition written to honor the university's 100th year. Aaron Neville was the featured artist for the Centennial Concert held at the Cannon Center for the Performing Arts. Lawrence Edwards conducted the University Choir with Mr. Neville who sang with one of our students. Former presidents of the university, retired faculty and staff, and distinguished officials from the city, county, and state attended. The evening was electric with beautiful sounds, excited performers, and the thrill of the launch of the whirlwind of activities for the year to celebrate our centennial.

Cutting the cake for the 100th anniversary celebration with Dr. Rosie Phillips Bingham, Vice President of Student Affairs, on my left and Tyler DeWitt, President of the Student Government Association, on my right.

The Scheidt School of Music joined with the Department of Theatre and Dance to present *Phantom of the Opera* by Andrew Lloyd Webber and Tim Rice. We were the only university permitted to perform the opera. We gained the permission because of the reputation of our music program. The *Phantom of the Opera* music was so difficult and exhausting to sing that we had two different casts to perform it.

Our capital campaign was called "Empowering the Dream." We had a grand party for the culmination of the Centennial year and the fundraising campaign. The party in the University Center was hosted by Campaign Co-chairs Charles and Judy Burkett. Mayor A C Wharton of Memphis, Mayor Mark Luttrell of Shelby County, and all of the Board of Visitor chairs and members attended. Since I had announced in April that I would retire from the university at the end of June, we combined the end of our Centennial Anniversary year celebration with a "good-bye" event for me.

Judy Burkett complimented me on my leadership, courage, and unwavering commitment, words I shall always treasure. When the band played my favorite, "Walking in Memphis" theme song by Marc Cohen, I was brought to tears. A touching video of remarks from students, faculty, and staff credited me with imagination, insight, and boldness. I received far more accoldates than I could accept, but I enjoyed them, anyway.

As a first-generation college student, I was passionate about making certain that students had scholarship opportunities. Three Dr. Shirley C. Raines scholarships were established, one by Brad and Dina Martin for graduate students in education. Another scholarship was established by Harry and Beth Smith to honor my parents, Evelyn Irene Raines and James Athel Raines, a most gratifying and touching distinction for their lives. A third scholarship was established in my name by the Wilson Family Foundation for students pursuing degrees in hospitality and resort management.

Mother and my son, Brian, at my inauguration as President of the
University of Memphis.

AN ENDING DATE REQUIRED

When I almost simultaneously experienced two life-altering events, one of great joy and one of great despair, I knew my time was over as president of the University of Memphis. I felt the great joy a grandchild can bring when my granddaughter Riley Marie Smith was born. I longed to be in East Tennessee, near my son and his family. Later, my grandson Bryson was born, making proximity to my son's family even more appealing. So, Bob and I bought our retirement home in Oak Ridge.

Then, I was filled with great despair, and life changed dramatically and immediately when my brother David told me he would die without a very risky medical procedure. For him to be approved for a left ventricle assist device, and if successful, a new heart, a family member had to be living within a few minutes of Vanderbilt hospital and to be present every day with him to meet with doctors and those who cared for him. I knew my sainted parents would expect me, the big sister, to be that family member. Others in the family had responsibilities that they could not leave on a daily basis. I could leave. So I submitted my resignation effective June 30, 2013, and temporarily moved to Nashville to be with my brother. Unfortunately, in November of 2013, David died at Vanderbilt Hospital from complications of receiving the "thought to be" life-saving device until he could receive a heart transplant, which never occurred.

THANKS FOR THE MEMORIES

The combined celebration of the success of the capital campaign and my goodbye was bittersweet. Bob, my long-suffering husband, had thought he was going to be in Memphis for five years but stayed for 12. He had gone to one too many receptions, one too many graduations, and one too many operas. He was thrilled to hear the news of my decision to step down from the presidency, but he knew saying "goodbye" was going to be more difficult than saying "hello." Bob also experienced a special moment during the combination Centennial Celebration and good-bye party. Dina Martin, the beautiful and talented wife of Brad Martin, a former chairman of the Board of Visitors, sang her rendition of the song "At Last" to Bob.

Memories Recalled

Recounting the milestones of my 12 year career as president of the University of Memphis caused me to reflect about the herculean projects we undertook. Writing about the projects made me realize that the people who worked with me were extraordinary leaders. In researching and writing this book, I reviewed countless documents and video clips, and I talked with friends, faculty members, donors, alumni, staff, and students. Overwhelmed by the emotions of reliving our times and conjuring up the memories of our great work together, I found that words seem insufficient to thank people adequately.

Drawn by the transformation that education brings, even the ups and downs, the daily pleasures and problems were far greater than I could have imagined when I first said, "Hello" to the University of Memphis. There always was a whirlwind of activity led by the executive level team members, my office staff, and many dynamic students. Now, more than ever, I appreciate those student government presidents who had some idealistic and far-flung ideas, with their tearful, joyful, long-suffering, fun, and beautiful moments. The great ideas that came from our academic community, the deep beliefs in the value of what we were doing, and the rewards on graduation day always, always outdistanced the sacrifices.

Sincerely, deeply, I want to thank everyone with a title, those without a title, givers with a few dollars, and donors with millions, you made it possible for us to lead our university confidently ahead. No president could have been more fortunate than I to have a President's Council and leadership boards supporting the university. They included the National Alumni Association, Foundation Board, Herff Trust, Tiger Clubs, Ambassadors, the Board of Visitors and supportive chancellors, staff, and regents. We benefited from intelligent discussions, forthright strategies, and solid support systems. We enjoyed the drive and dedication of true leaders, on campus and off. Our leadership team was right most of the time, and we usually enjoyed each other's company. When we went astray, we made a course correction. We praised our peers, celebrated those who reported to us and championed, always championed, the students.

MY GRADUATION FROM BEING UNIVERSITY PRESIDENT

Perhaps now is the time to probe my memory and recall graduation speeches I have heard. Some people say graduation speeches are supposed to be forgotten, but some speakers I will not forget. Among the most memorable were Assisi Foundation Director Jan Young, who quoted Mother Teresa; Board of Visitors Chairman Larry Papasan, who with tears in his eyes thanked his Mississippi upbringing; philanthropist Jim Ayers, who told about the professor who saved him from dropping out of college; Plough Foundation Chair Diane Rudner, who looked out over the audience and challenged graduates to change the world. Perhaps, one of the most quoted graduation phrases came from Senator

Lamar Alexander, who quoted Alex Haley's six famous words, "Find the good and praise it." And, we did. We looked every day for the good of our students, faculty, staff, alumni, and community supporters. And, we praised them, expected more, and they responded.

Dr. Scott Morris said in the graduation speech he delivered, "Pulling yourself up by your own bootstraps is a crazy idea. No one does it alone, no one." And growing up, being a student, becoming a teacher, professor, and later an administrator, even a university president, I was never alone. My wish for every leader is to have someone who will pull you up and onward for the greater good you can achieve.

A determined, driven, sentimental, and ambitious leader, I was ambitious for our university and scared to death that we would miss an opportunity. Somehow, the spirit of the place surrounded me and kept me pushing. I enjoyed the uphill climb, and always looked ahead, counting on the university's bright future. Under the leaders that followed me, Interim President Brad Martin, and now President M. David Rudd, the bright future continues.

Waving goodbye to the campus and to my role as the 11th President of the University of Memphis.

Chapter 14

LESSONS FOR LEADERSHIP: SAY "YES" TO LEADERSHIP

PERCEIVING, BEHAVING, BECOMING

Perceiving, Behaving, Becoming was the title of a book that was assigned reading in one of my undergraduate courses. While the book was enlightening, at the end of the semester on a tight budget to pay my fees, I sold the book back to the bookstore for a few dollars. However, I worked in the bookstore and in the return bin I found the very copy I had sold back. When my next paycheck arrived, I bought back my own copy of the book. Obviously, it was significant to read articles by famous psychologists, such as Kelley, Rogers, Maslow, and Combs, but it is the title that has stuck with me over the years.

Perceiving, behaving and becoming are the steps each leader must take. *Perceiving the role of leader* is best when it comes from serving under and observing closely the leaders we most want to emulate. Reading about the leadership role, studying the expectations of the job, and reconciling our desires for leadership with what the job requires are important perception steps.

Behaving the role of leader means that in every position, special assignment, group project, volunteer role, or first leadership job, we must strive to behave like the best leaders we know. And, even when we fall short of behaving at our best, we must have the desire to continually improve.

The process of *becoming a leader* is never ending. In each new position, there are changes in expectations and challenges far beyond what we perceived when we took the job. Continuing to learn and grow from the experiences means we are still in the "becoming" stage. There is no actual end to the becoming process. While we may reach the pinnacle of our career journey in time and title, the process of becoming will be required for whatever next steps we take in our life.

Do You Want to Take the Next Leadership Step?

The question is: Do you want to become a leader and take the next steps to realize your ambition? In one of my sessions at a conference, a participant gave me all the reasons she did not want the role of a director. Then, I asked, "Then why are you in this leadership session?" In reality, people need to investigate whether or not they are a good fit to be a leader, but "desire" is crucial. You must want to lead to confidently say "yes" to leadership.

Are you a good fit for leadership? Over the course of my leadership journey, I have guided a lot of potential leaders to decide their best course of action. For some, it was applying for a leadership job.

For others, it was helping them to know they were ready. An honest appraisal is needed. You can analyze your strengths and weaknesses for leadership through a variety of means. For example, you might consult with successful leaders. Some find leadership conferences, as *Leadercast*, help you identify "leaders worth following." Whatever avenue you choose, plan to attend good leadership training that requires you to be analytical, emotional, and ambitious. Analyze your strengths and leadership personality and discover how others perceive you.

Many training programs require you to take the *Myers-Briggs Type Indicator* (MBTI), a personality type assessment based on the work of Carl Jung. Guidance about your personality type can help you become more effective in working relationships, communications, and career decisions.

Another helpful tool was developed by Tom Rath, *Strengths Finder 2.0,* with an on-line test from the Gallup Corporation that leads to an action planning guide. Among the strengths required of leaders is emotional intelligence. In *Emotional Intelligence 2.0,* Travis Bradberry and Jean Greaves describe an instrument they developed to measure emotional intelligence and provide strategies to improve emotional intelligence for both personal and professional success.

Your leadership voice is dependent upon your personality, strengths, and willingness to work toward improvement to become the leader you want to be. To determine your leadership voice, I suggest the work of Jeremie Kubicek and Steve Cockram in *5 Voices: How to Communicate Effectively with Everyone You Lead.* They explain five leadership voices: the Pioneer, the Connector, the Creative, the Guardian, and the Nurturer. Examining the five voices helps the leader determine his or her voice and the different voices of their team members. They understand how and why their team members interact in certain ways. The group can learn to function more cohesively and effectively when they know the characteristics of the voices of their team members.

Another tool is the *360 Leadership Assessment* from the Center for Creative Leadership. I used the assessment in two major leadership positions. The instrument solicits anonymous feedback from the people who report to you on your job performance from multiple perspectives. The goal is to become aware of how others perceive you and in so doing develop goals that help you improve your performance as a leader.

READINESS TO LEAD

When you have completed your research and assessments, you will feel that you are right for leadership. You are up for the challenge, excited by the possibilities, and willing to learn. What should you do next?

Say, "Yes." Start your leadership journey. Apply for jobs you qualify for that involve team leadership. You may take a job in your present workplace or strike out on a new adventure in a different city and try your wings. Whatever path you take, there will be rewards, challenges, successes, and disappointments. As the leader, you can make a difference and shape a better future for yourself, your family, and for your employees by saying "Yes" to taking your own leadership journey.

EMOTIONALLY READY AND EQUIPPED TO LEAD

From the story of my uncommon journey and the leadership lessons highlighted, I hope you reflected on your leadership potential.

Answering the questions in appendix one can lead to more leadership insights. The tools I mentioned from the Myers-Briggs to the 360 Leadership Assessment are just that–"tools." My story, your reflections, and your self-assessment along with these leadership tools can provide you with more depth of understanding about leadership requirements and your own strengths.

The most essential understandings come from your own life and previous leadership experiences and positions you have held, whether or not you have followed a common path or yours has been an uncommon leadership journey, too. Caring deeply about your chosen field, believing in great principles that feed your soul and make you swell with pride, a vision for a future in which your leadership makes a difference – these are the very stepping stones for your journey. Recall the Joseph Campbell quote: "If you can see your path laid out in front of you, step by step, you know it's not your path. Your own path you make with every step you take. That's why it's your path."

APPENDIXES

NOTES AND QUESTIONS
FOR REFLECTION

Consider your leadership journey. Answer the questions based on chapters 2-14, reflect on your experiences and the possibilities for your future.

Chapter 2: Who's in Charge?

Recall your first day on the job when you felt like you were in charge. What did you do to gain the trust of those who reported to you?

Who is your professional colleague on whom you always count?

Recall the last career move you made. How did you begin your working relationship with those who had more expertise than you?

How has your feeling of being "in charge" changed over time?

Chapter 3: A Crisis in Leadership

Would you have accepted the department chair position or a similar position in your organization?

How do you think the announcement should be made about a new department chair, supervisor, or manager?

What would you have done differently in the meeting with the difficult faculty member?

Additional Notes: Several times in my career, I was the youngest university professor, least in rank and title. Yet those experiences taught me to respect older professionals, work on improving communication, recognize my limitations, and view problems from others' perspectives. Most importantly, I learned how opportunity is not always some grand door opening. It simply may be the willingness to say, "Yes, I'll take the job," when others have turned it down.

Chapter 4: Moving On and Moving Up

What would you have done in the situation if a supervisor had treated you in a similar humiliating way?

Are women the only leaders who feel this type of humiliation?

What are the human resources options, and what are the ones you would be willing to pursue to resolve a problem with your supervisor?

Chapter 5: Be Yourself, Your Best Self

What advice would you give a friend who is applying for a position of authority?

What are the major challenges you and your colleague leaders face in your organization on a daily basis and long-term?

Recall the "mugging" ceremony for acknowledging individual work. Do you have some suggestions for an activity that would acknowledge successful teams?

Would you have accepted the two simultaneous positions?

What would you have replied to the accusation of "superwoman" or "superman" complex?

Chapter 6: What Are the Chances?

In an interview, what are some questions you would expect to be asked if the interviewers are taking you seriously.

Have you ever felt people were just going through the motions in an interview with you? Is there any way to turn that situation around?

What is your leadership philosophy? Sometimes people determine their philosophy by considering leaders with whom they enjoy working. Who are some leaders you have known who have a good leadership philosophy?

How would you find out about the organization you want to join?

What are you willing to fight for that shows your toughness and your knowledge?

Chapter 7: Walking in Memphis

Were you the candidate expected to win the position you hold now?

What were your early days like in your new position?

Who gave you advice and was it helpful for your early success?

In your present position, who introduced you and to whom were you introduced?

If you have a spouse, what role does your spouse or partner play in your professional life?

If you were accepting your dream position, what would you say in your first speech?

Chapter 8: Building Leadership

Recall people in your workplace whom you trusted and were people of integrity. How did you know they were trustworthy and had integrity?

Remember a situation in which people did not get along. Do you know why? What did their communication reveal to you about them?

What would you do if you were in my situation and learned that two highly capable people were not getting along with each other?

Have you ever given someone you supervised a second chance? How did it work out?

What is the difference between cooperation and collaboration?

Chapter 9: Creating the Structure for Success

While a university is not like a corporation in structure, standards of practice shape all organizations. What is the corporate structure in which you work?

What is the structure of a professional association to which you belong?

What is a motto from a civic organization to which you belong that has great meaning for you?

Recall the vision and mission statements of the organization. Does the motto support those statements or serve as the inspiration for the work of your organization?

If you are self-employed, which professional organizations, trade shows, or personal contacts have helped you learn something new?

Write your own personal leadership motto. If you considered more than one motto, try them out with a trusted colleague.

Chapter 10: Resourcefulness and Perseverance for Legendary Building Projects

Think about the campuses where you have studied or places where you have worked. Who designed the buildings, and whom were they meant to serve?

When new initiatives are undertaken, whether buildings or academic programs, or a new product launched, what facets deserve the leader's attention?

When you recall your work experience, what team projects were sustained for a long period of time? What was needed to sustain the efforts to completion? What expertise, level of tenaciousness, social, and political contacts were necessary to accomplish your project's desired end?

How do you honor people who are contributors to society philanthropically?

Many people are contributors by their volunteer efforts, as examples to others and by using their influence, but they may lack the financial means to contribute to an organization. How should those who lack the financial means be honored?

Are there any parallels in university administration to corporate life, to a civic or professional organization to which you belong?

Chapter 11: Beyond the Boundaries

Consider the highest level administrator above you who must approve a project you are leading. If you have contact with her or him, how do you handle the informal opportunities to interact? If you must schedule all contacts, who are the other employees or representatives you would like to accompany you?

If you were redesigning the building where you work, what would you do differently? Consider where it is located, how employees interact with the "built" space and the green spaces. What would you change to make it more conducive to work, safer, more efficient, and a place you want to work on a daily basis?

If you are involved with non-profit organizations, how do you research their focus, grant-making processes, and who the influencers in the foundation or organization are?

Do you have the administrative skill to negotiate a complicated deal? Who are the people you would put on your team to ensure the success of a deal or a project?

Chapter 12: Athletics in Perspective

Which sports capture your attention and the attention of your community?

As a leader, have you ever had training on how to handle a press conference?

What are the advantages and disadvantages of asking people you know if you can give their names and contact information for reference checks?

What are the pros and cons of private versus public searches for very public leaders?

Do you have any famous or flamboyant people in your organization? Do they influence your organization's operation? How do you deal with them?

If you were going to interview for a high-profile position, what would your equivalent "plan to become champions" be?

When you do not know enough about a person or a topic, how do you go about obtaining the needed information?

Do you have experience working with legal professionals associated with your work?

Chapter 13: Saying "Goodbye" Is Harder than Saying "Hello"

Recall a position where you felt especially close to team members with whom you worked. What made your team function well?

If you were asked to write a speech for a graduation ceremony, what would you tell the graduates?

What family or life changes have made you rethink your career?

If someone named a scholarship for you, what would be the area and what would you want the winners to know about you?

Chapter 14: Lessons for Leadership, Say "Yes" to Leadership

In many ways, all of Chapter 14 is a series of reflective questions with additional thoughts and advice. The most obvious questions - Are you ready to say "yes" to leadership? Are you ready to take the next bold step on your leadership journey?

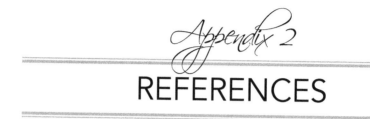

REFERENCES

American Council on Education. 2017. *American College President Study.* Washington, DC: American Council on Education.

Beaudine, B., & Dooley, T. 2009. *The Power of Who! You Already Know Everyone You Need to Know.* New York: Center Street.

Bond, B., Sherman, J., & Breland, F. W. 2012. *University of Memphis: The Campus History Series.* Charleston, SC: Arcadia Publishing.

Bradberry, T., & Greaves, J. 2009. *Emotional Intelligence 2.0.* San Diego: Talent Smart.

Campbell, J. (retrieved from website: httpps://www.sapphyr.net/smallgems/quotes – author – josephcampbell.htm).

Cohen, M. 1991. Song - *Walking in Memphis.* Atlantic Records.

Combs, A. W. (Ed.). 1962. *Perceiving, Behaving, Becoming.* Washington, DC: National Education Association.

Cummings, D. 2015. *The Sensational Salesman: A Second Chance Story.* Bloomington, IN: Balboa Press.

Egan, K. 1986. *Teaching as Storytelling.* Chicago: The University of Chicago Press.

Haley, A. *Quotes by Alex Haley: "Find the good and praise it."* (retrieved from https://www.goodreads.com/quotes).

Kubicek, J., & Cockram, S. 2016. *5 Voices: How to Communicate Effectively with Everyone You Lead.* Hoboken, NJ: Wiley Press.

Leadercast. (website: https//live.leadercast.com).

360 Leadership Assessment. *Center for Creative Leadership.* Greensboro, NC: (website: https://www.ccl.org/lead-it-yourself-solutions/benchmarks-360-assessment-suite/).

Myers. J. 2014. *Hitting the Curve Balls: How Crisis Can Strengthen and Grow Your Business.* New York: Morgan James Publishing.

Rath, T. 2007. *Strengths Finder, 2.0.* New York: Gallup Press.

Roosevelt, E., *Virtues for Life,* (retrieved from: www.virtuesfor-life.com/10-inspiring-quotes-by-eleanor-roosevelt/).

Shakespeare, W. Hamlet. (retrieved from www. enotes.com/ shakespeare's quotes).

The Chronicle of Higher Education, Washington, DC.

The Commercial Appeal, Memphis, TN.

The Myers-Briggs Type Indicator, (MBTI), (website: *www.mbtionline.com).*

PHOTOGRAPHIC CREDITS

Photo 1: My first home where my family lived until I was in the seventh grade. (Family photograph)

Photo 2: The house our family moved into when my father bought a farm. (Family photograph)

Photo 3: My first day of school walking down the steps of our sharecropper farmhouse. (Family photograph)

Photo 4: My two brothers and me, David Raines (L) and Carey Raines (R). (Family photograph)

Photo 5: Mrs. Frances Hooks, me, my husband Bob Canady, and Dr. Hooks, legendary civil rights leader in the nation and a religious leader in the community. (Courtesy of Mark Stansbury)

Photo 6: My husband, Bob Canady, and I ride together in the homecoming parade. (Rhonda Cosentino, Courtesy of University of Memphis)

Photo 7: A proud day in their lives. Father and Mother dressed for a lunch with the governor before my inauguration ceremony. (Courtesy of University of Memphis)

Photo 8: The academic crest that helped modernize the image of the university. (Linda Bonnin, Courtesy of University of Memphis)

Photo 9: Tennessee Governor Bill Haslam and I discussing higher education issues (Courtesy of Governor's Office.)

Photo 10: Impressive bronze statue of mascot Tom the Tiger unveiled in front of the new University Center. (Rhonda Cosentino, Courtesy of University of Memphis)

Photo 11: The grand celebration for the opening of the FedEx Institute of Technology. (Courtesy of University of Memphis)

Photo 12: The Law School Building renovation was unveiled at a gala event. (Lindsey Lissau, Courtesy of University of Memphis)

Photo 13: Press conference announcing the University had acquired the rights to the Lambuth University property. (Rhonda Cosentino, Courtesy of University of Memphis)

Photo 14: Fans enjoy the Liberty Bowl and Tiger Lane while awaiting the team's march through the crowd. (Courtesy of the Autozone Liberty Bowl)

Photo 15: Educating young children started my career journey, and I never lost the joy of being with them. Here I am singing with the children at Campus School. (Rhonda Cosentino, Courtesy of University of Memphis)

Photo 16: Speaking at an alumni event about students making a different on campus, in the community, and beyond. (Rhonda Cosentino, Courtesy of University of Memphis)

Photo 17: The courageous men and women of the Memphis State Eight who integrated the campus in 1959. 2012 unveiling of the historical marker commemorating the courage of the Memphis State Eight. (Courtesy of University of Memphis)

Photo 18: Cutting the cake for the 100th anniversary celebration with Dr. Rosie Phillips Bingham, Vice President of Student Affairs, on my left and Tyler DeWitt, President of the Student Government Association, on my right. (Courtesy of the University of Memphis)

Photo 19: Mother and my son, Brian, at my inauguration as President of the University of Memphis. (Courtesy of the University of Memphis)

Photo 20: Waving goodbye to the campus and to my role as the 11th President of the University of Memphis. (Courtesy of the University of Memphis)

Appendix 4

ACKNOWLEDGMENTS

Thank you, family, friends, and colleagues who helped me develop as a leader on my "uncommon journey." Please accept my apologies for any persons inadvertently omitted from the acknowledgment lists.

Special acknowledgments to editors Don Barksdale and Carolyn Krause. For background information, Carol Crown, David Cox, Greg Russell, Jane Hooker, Jeanine Rakow, Linda Bonnin, Lindsey Lissau, Mark Stansbury, Pat Faudree, Rhonda Cosentino, Rosetta Sandidge, Sheila Hall, Sonja Mason, Susan Elliott, and Tony Poteet.

To the governors and chancellors who appointed me and supported the University of Memphis: The Honorable Donald Kenneth Sundquist; The Honorable Phillip Norman Bredesen; The Honorable Bill Haslam; executive director of Tennessee Higher Education Commission, Richard Rhoda; Tennessee Board of Regents chancellors Charles Manning and John Morgan; executive director of facilities Jerry Preston, vice chancellor Paula Short, and to all the TBR staff. To Board of Regents chairs Jack Fishman, Bob Thomas,

Fran Markum, and Greg Duckett; also to regents Bill Watkins, Dr. Maxine Smith, and Judy Gooch.

This list contains the names of friends and colleagues from programs, schools, colleges, universities, and publishers. Thank you to Ann Brown, Anne Hayes, Beverly Bond, Bill Katzenmeyer, Bob Gilstap, Carol Danehower, Carolyn Williams, Connie Duckett, Connie Hines, Dianne Papasan, Glenda Shorb, Gwen Winder, Howard Johnston, Janann Sherman, Jim Hellums, Jim Paul, Joan Isenberg-Samuels, John DeAtley, Kathy Charner, Katie Crow, Kay Grant, Larry Rood, Leah Curry-Rood, Lucia Gilliland, Marshall Brooks, Mary Ann Vimont, Melba Johnson, Michael Hagge, Moira Logan, Pam Cash, Pat Allen, Phyllis Betts, Randal Rushing, Retha Higgs, Retia Scott Walker, Rhoda-Gale Pollack, Richard Janikowski, Rita Sparks, Rob Shapiro, Rosemary Waters, Rosetta Sandidge, Sandra Brown Turner, Sharon Brennan, Sharon Hayes, and Susan Copeland.

Special appreciation to the President's Council members during my tenure, in order of service: Provost Ralph Faudree, interim provost Thomas Nenon, provost M. David Rudd; vice presidents for Business and Finance Raymond Pipkin, Charles Lee, David Zettergren; vice president for Student Affairs, Don Carson and Rosie Phillips Bingham; vice president Communications, Marketing, Alumni, and Government Relations Kevin Roper; reorganized to vice president Communications and Marketing, Bob Eoff and Linda Bonnin; vice president of Development and Alumni Relations Julie Johnson; athletic directors R.C. Johnson and Tom Bowen; vice president Information Technology and CIO James Penrod, Doug Hurley, and Ellen Watson; and executive assistants to the president Janet Mitchell, Martha Alberg, David Cox, and Mark Stansbury.

To staff members in all offices on campus, especially president's office staff members who served at various times during my tenure: Arlene Abernathy, Stephanie Beasley, Charlotte Bray, La Torya Ceruti, Susan Elliott, Kelli Leubbe, Janet Mitchell, Jeanine Rakow, Shelby Tate, and part-time employees, work-study, and graduate students.

Affirmative action officers, Michelle Banks and Karen Weddle-West; auditor, Byron Morgan; campus police chief Bruce Harber; university legal counsel, Sheryl Lipman.

Deans at the University of Memphis from 2001-2013: Arts and Sciences, Peter Bridson, Henry Kurtz, Thomas Nenon; Cecil C. Humphreys College of Law, Don Polden, James Smoot, Kevin Smith, Peter Letsou; Education, Nathan Essex, interim John Schifani, Rick Hovda, interim Mike Hamrick, Donald Wagner, interim Ernest Rakow; Fogelman College of Business and Economics, John Pepin, Rajiv Grover (School of Accountancy and the School of Hospitality and Resort Management were a part of the Fogelman College in 2013 at my retirement); Herff College of Engineering, Richard Warder, Richard Sweigard; Loewenberg School of Nursing, Toni Bargagliotti, Marjorie Luttrell, Lin Zhan; School of Communications and Fine Arts, Richard Ranta (School of Music included); School of Communications Sciences and Disorders, Maurice Mendel; School of Public Health, Lisa Klesges; Graduate School, Diane Horgan, Karen Weddle-West; University College and Extended Programs, Dan Lattimore; and University Library, Sylverna Ford.

Special appreciation to the vice provosts: Andrew Myers, research and sponsored programs, who organized the Research Foundation Board with support from Deborah Hernandez; Karen Weddle-West, academic affairs; Shannon Blanton, undergraduate studies ; Tom Nenon, academic affairs, interim provost and dean of the College of Arts and Sciences.

Directors of the Centers of Excellence; the FedEx Institute of Technology; engaged scholarship award winners; president's award winners from faculty and staff; research award winners; and Willard Sparks Eminent Faculty Award winners.

Faculty and Staff Senate presidents: Thomas Banning, Jeffrey Berman, David Ciscel, Reginald Green, Wade Jackson, Kenneth Lambert, Sheryl Maxwell, Edward Perry, John Petry, Lawrence Pivnik, Patricia Stevens, and Stanley (Ed) Stevens; Staff Senate presidents, Susan Babb, Hugh Busby, Virginia Huss, Vicki Peters, and Pamela Williams.

Board of Visitors Founder Robert F. Fogelman; Board of Visitors chairs in order of service - Willard Sparks, interim chair John Kelley, Larry Papasan, R. Brad Martin, Charles Burkett, Tom Watson. Special appreciation to: Ben Bryant for advising the FedEx Institute of Technology; Harry Smith and Stephen Reynolds for chairing the investment committees; Hilliard Crews for the Crews Center; Rudi E. Scheidt for the Music School; and John Stokes for assistance with the Law School Building;

Board of Visitors and University of Memphis Foundation Board of Trustees Members and their families at the time of my retirement: Julie Johnson, executive director; Larry Bunch, auditor. Members: A C Wharton, Anise Belz, Amy Rhodes, Art Gilliam, Benjamin Cullen Bryant, Bill Watkins, Burns Landess, Carolyn Hardy, Carolyn Williams-Bennett, David Bronczek, David Ferraro, David Kustoff, David Perdue, David Porter, David Wedaman, Diane Vescovo, Douglas Edwards, Elliot Perry, Floyd Tyler, Frank Flautt, Fred Hodges, Gary Shorb, Greg Duckett, Harry Smith, Helen Gronauer, Hilliard Crews, James McGehee, Jim Vining, Joe

Orgill, John Farris, John Stokes, Laurie Tucker, Mark Luttrell, Mike Bruns, Pat Kerr Tigrett, Paulette Delk, Phil Trenary, Rick Spell, Rita Sparks, Robert Fogelman, Rudi E. Scheidt, Stephan Smith, Stephen Reynolds, Thomas Kadien, Tom Watson, Trish Calvert Ring, and Willie Gregory.

Donors who established and supported special programs, including Burt Bornblum, Billie and Tommie Dunavant, the Felt and Loewenberg families, Harry Feinstone, Jabie and Helen Hardin, and Tommie Pardue.

Longest serving trustees of the Herb Herff Trust: George Cates, R. Eugene Smith, and William Rudner.

National Alumni Association for Alumni and Friends: Tammy Hedges, executive director; selected leaders - Allie Prescott, Amy Amundsen, Andrew Bailey, Anita Vaughn, Barbara Prescott, Ben Watkins, Bob Byrd, Bobby Wharton, Butch Childers, Carolyn Hardy, Darrell Cobbins, Dana Gabrion, Dawn Graeter, Deanie Parker, Harold Byrd, Harold Graeter, Jeff Farmer, Jim Strickland, John Koski, John Lawrence, Judy Long, Kim Barnett, Mark Long, Norma Upshur, Paul Jewel, Renee De Gutis, Richard Glassman, Robert Wright, Ron Hart, Wei Chin.

Athletes, fans, and donors to Tiger Athletic Scholarship Funds and to organizers and sponsors of the sports booster clubs. The most active at the time of my retirement were the "M" Club, Highland Hundred, Rebounders, and the Fastbreak Club.

Athletic Ambassadors at the time of my retirement: Al LaRocca, Alan Graf, Anfernee Hardaway, Anne Stokes, Audrea Edwards, Benjamin Bryant, Bernadette Rice, Betty Moore, Bill Morris, Billy Bond, Billy Dunavant, Billy Orgel, Bob Byrd, Brenda Flautt, Carol LaRocca, Charlotte Hodges, Daniel Feinstone, Dave Bronczek,

Debbi Rose, Dina Martin, Doris Hillhouse, Doug Edwards, Elaine Springer, Elkan Scheidt, Evelyn Echols, Frank Flautt, Fred Hodges, Fred Smith, Gary Rosenberg, George Johnson, Gina Wiertelak, Glen Brown, Glenna Flautt, Harold Byrd, Hilliard Crews, Jack Jones, Jack Moore, Janet January, Jennifer Russell, Jessie Boyd, Jim Hillhouse, Jim Wiertelak, John Stokes, Jr., Judy Baird, Karen Fields Issacman, Kathryn Feinstone, Ken Issacman, Ken Lenoir, Lauren Pickens, Laurie Scheidt, Lenny Feller, Marian Bruns, Marsha Cohn, Martha Bryant, Mike Bruns, Mike Rose, Rhonda Feller, Rick Spell, Rita Sparks, Robin Orgel, Robin Watson, Ron Terry, Sandra Jones, Sandy Lenoir, Sandy Spell, Susan Graf, Tom Watson, Tommie Dunavant, Valerie Brown, Wynoka Terry.

Foundation Directors: Jan Young, Assisi; Jim and Janet Ayers, Ayers Foundation; Diane Rudner, Plough Foundation; Pit and Barbara Hyde, Teresa Sloyan, Hyde Family Foundation; Betty Moore, Bob Wilson, Carole West, Kemmons Wilson, Jr., and Spence Wilson, Kemmons Wilson Foundation.

Elected officials, especially, Mayors of Memphis and of Shelby County, A C Wharton, Jim Rout, Jim Strickland, Mark Luttrell, and Willie Herenton. Elected officials in the General Assembly of the State of Tennessee and to our United States Senators and Representatives.